THE HERO

IN HISTORY

THE HERO IN HISTORY

A Study in Limitation and Possibility

SIDNEY HOOK

BEACON PRESS · BOSTON

International Standard Book Number: 0–8070–5081–4

19   18   17   16   15   14   13   12   11   10

To
Benjie and Susan,
no hero-worshippers

Contents

INTRODUCTION

I THE HERO AS EVENT AND PROBLEM, 3. 1 Leadership in the Modern World, 2 The Cultivation of the Hero, 3 The Hero as a Child of Crisis, 4 The Hero and the Philosopher of History, 5 Psychological Roots of Hero-Interest

II THE HEROES OF THOUGHT, 27. 1 Literature, Music, and Painting, 2 Philosophy and Science, 3 Religion, 4 The Historical Hero

III THE INFLUENCE OF MONARCHS, 42. 1 The Character of Rulers and Historical Conditions, 2 Some Striking Correlations, 3 Royalty by Right of Gametes, 4 Interpretations of Wood's Findings

IV SOCIAL DETERMINISM: HEGEL AND SPENCER, 59. 1 The Hegelian World-Spirit, 2 The Common Assumptions of Determinism, 3 The Spencerian Formula

V SOCIAL DETERMINISM: ORTHO-
DOX MARXISM, 75. *1 Empirical Ele-
ments, 2 Engels and the Mysticism of Dialectics,
3 Plechanov and Madame Pompadour, 4 The Conflict Between Monism and Evidence*

VI THE FRAMEWORK OF HEROIC
ACTION, 102. *1 The Heritage of So-
cial Determinism, 2 Heroic Action and Historical
Alternatives, 3 The Hero as Puppet*

VII "IF" IN HISTORY, 119. *1 Drouet's
Cart and the Fall of France, 2 The
Invasion of England, 3 The Persian Victory at
Marathon, 4 Winston Churchill on Lee's Victory
at Gettysburg, 5 The Fanciful "IF" and Scientific
"IF," 6 The Hazards of Prophecy*

VIII THE CONTINGENT AND
THE UNFORESEEN, 137. *1 The
Variety of Historical Perspectives, 2 The Mean-
ings of Contingency, 3 The Limits of Contingency, 4 The Lost Chances of History*

IX THE EVENTFUL MAN AND THE
EVENT-MAKING MAN, 151. *1 De-
fining the Hero, 2 Eventful and Event-Making
Personalities, 3 Constantine and Jefferson, 4 The
Uneventful Period, 5 Robespierre and Justinian, 6
The Hero, the Machine, and the Social Class, 7 The
Illusion of Eventfulness, 8 Some Eventful Women:
Cleopatra, Theodora, Catherine II*

X *THE RUSSIAN REVOLUTION: A TEST CASE, 184. 1 The Influence of the October Revolution, 2 Was the October Revolution Historically Inevitable? 3 Lenin as an Eventful Man or Historical Hero, 4 A World Without Lenin, 5 Lenin's Political Portrait*

XI *THE HERO AND DEMOCRACY, 229. 1 Can a Democracy Trust Heroes? 2 The Hero as a Demagogue, 3 Heroes and Delegated Powers, 4 The Democratic Philosophy of the Hero, 5 The Critics of Democracy: Mosca, Pareto, and Michels*

XII *LAW, FREEDOM, AND HUMAN ACTION, 246. 1 The Scope of Historical Laws, 2 Degrees of Social Necessity, 3 Responsibility and Freedom, 4 The Alternatives Before Us*

INDEX, 269

Introduction

THE TITLE of this book indicates its subject matter, not a special philosophy of history. It could with as much justice have been entitled "The Limits of the Hero in History." That, too, would tell what the book is about and not what we believe about it. What we believe about it is detailed in the book. The reader is begged not to infer it from the title alone.

That history is made by men and women is no longer denied except by some theologians and mystical metaphysicians. And even they are compelled indirectly to acknowledge this commonplace truth, for they speak of historical personages as "instruments" of Providence, Justice, Reason, Dialectic, the *Zeitgeist*, or Spirit of the Times. Men agree more readily about the consequences of the use of "instruments" in history than they do about the ultimate ends "instruments" allegedly serve, or the first causes by which they are allegedly determined.

Consequences are difficult to establish; human intentions more so. In principle, where there is a desire to know the truth, we can intelligently answer questions about our intentions. But there can be no scientific agreement about the intentions of capitalized abstractions and the determinations of first causes, for in respect to them we cannot make the same assumptions about meaning, evidence, and truth.

We know that the ravages of Attila accelerated the decline of the Roman Empire. We cannot be so sure as some of his pious victims that he was "the scourge of God"; nor altogether convinced, like some modern scholars, that he was the end effect of a chain of causes whose first link was forged in the climatic variations of China.

We know that Hitler gave the signal which plunged all the six continents of the world into war. It is doubtful that, as one initiate in God's mysteries recently proclaimed, Hitler and other tyrants are "instruments of Divine Justice, chastening a people who had departed from the way of truth"; or, as others have it, that he is merely the result of the basic cause of our time of troubles—the failure to bring the social relations of production into line with the expanding forces of production.

Let men be instruments, if the metaphor is pleasing. But let it also be remembered that instruments may be used for various and sometimes totally different purposes. And man is also an instrument who has something to say about what these purposes shall be. The Purpose he presumably serves is to be construed from the purposes he himself sets and realizes. For men make history only when they have purposes.

Whatever men make, their making is always subject to certain conditions—whether it be a gun or a book, a war or revolution, another society or another man. Even most of the gods conceived by men create under the limitations of materials existing at the time they act. Any other kind of creation is a mystery to the credulous and an incoherent myth to the critical.

Every philosophy of history which recognizes that men can and do make their own history also concerns itself with the conditions under which it is made. It assesses in a broad and general way the relative weight, for a certain period, of the conditions under which men act and of their ideals, plans, and purposes. These ideals, plans, and purposes are causally rooted in the complex of conditions, but they take their meaning from some proposed *reworking* of conditions to bring them closer to human desire. The same theme is also involved in the specific inquiries of scientific historians. It is difficult to give a satisfactory account of what happened, how it happened, and why, without striking a plausible balance between the part men played and the conditioning scene which provided the materials, sometimes the rules, but never the plots of the dramas of human history. Philosophers have treated this question in the large; historians, in the small. The first have offered wholesale solutions usually in the interest of programs of action or hopes of salvation. The second have eschewed large-scale generalizations and cautiously gone from case to case. This is pre-eminently true of the role of the "great man" or "hero" in history.

What the analysis in the subsequent pages aims at is primarily a fruitful formulation of this fascinating problem. An attempt will be made to work out some generalizations of the types of situations and conditions in which we can justifiably attribute or deny casual influence to outstanding personalities. We are offering not a theory of history but a contribution to a theory of history, one which must be taken note of in any adequate account of human history.

S. H.

THE HERO

IN HISTORY

I *The Hero as Event and Problem*

THERE IS a perennial interest in heroes even when we outgrow the hero worship of youth. The sources of this interest are many and deep. But they vary in intensity and character from one historic period to another. In our own time interest in the words and acts of outstanding individuals has flared up to a point never reached before. The special reasons for this passionate concern in the ideas and deeds of the uncrowned heroes of our age are quite apparent. During a period of wars and revolutions, the fate of peoples seems to hang visibly on what one person, perhaps a few, decide. It is true that these special reasons reflect the dramatic immediacy of issues joined in battle, but there are other sources of interest which operate in less agonized times. We shall discuss both.

1. The basic fact that provides the material for interest in heroes is the indispensability of *leadership* in all social life, and in every major form of social organization. The controls over leadership, whether open or hidden, differ from society to society, but leaders are always at hand

3

—not merely as conspicuous symbols of state, but as centers of responsibility, decision, and action. There is a natural tendency to associate the leader with the results achieved under his leadership even when these achievements, good or bad, have resulted despite his leadership rather than because of it. Where many factors are at work, the fallacy of *post hoc, ergo propter hoc* has a fateful plausibility to the simple mental economy of the uncritical multitude as well as to impatient men of action. A Hoover will be held accountable for a depression whose seeds were planted long before his advent. A Baldwin will be considered safe and sane if no social catastrophe breaks out during his ministry, even if he has lit a slow-burning fuse to the European powder magazine.

In our own day, the pervasive influence of leadership on the daily life of entire populations need no longer be imputed. For good or evil, it is openly proclaimed, centrally organized, and continuously growing. The development of corporate economies under centralized governments in the major countries of the world is such that we may say, without exaggeration, that never before have so few men affected so many different fields at once. The key decisions in politics, economics, foreign relations, military and naval affairs, education, housing, public works, and relief, and—save in Anglo-America—in religion, art, literature, music, architecture, and science are made by a handful of national leaders, and frequently by one figure whose judgment and taste become the absolute laws of the land. The tremendous development of means of communication, which makes it possible to transmit decisions with the speed of light to every nook and corner, ensures an effectiveness of control never known before.

A Caesar, a Cromwell, a Napoleon could and did issue decrees in many fields. But these fields, administratively and functionally, were not knotted together so tightly as they are today. They could not exact universal obedience to their decrees, or even suppress criticism. Some avenues of escape could never be closed. Some asylums of the spirit remained inaccessible to their law-enforcement agencies. The active presence of conflicting tendencies not only in politics but in religion and philosophy, during the reign of absolute rulers of the past, showed that they could not box culture within the confines of their dogmas and edicts. Their failure was not for want of trying.

How different is the picture in much of the world to-day! A Hitler, a Stalin, a Mussolini not only can and do issue decrees in every field, from military organization to abstract art and music; such dictators enforce them one hundred per cent. Their decisions affect not only the possibilities of earning a livelihood—something not unique to totalitarian countries—but all education of children and adults, and both the direction and content of their nations' literature, art, and philosophy. They cannot, of course, command geniuses to rise in the fields they control but they can utterly destroy all nonconforming genius and talent. Through schools on every level, since literacy is a weapon; through the radio, which no one can escape if it is loud enough; through the press and cinema, to which men naturally turn for information and relaxation—they carry their education to the very "subconscious" of their people.

Silence and anonymity are no longer safeguards. All asylums of the spirit have been destroyed. The counsel of prudent withdrawal and disinterested curiosity from afar that Montaigne offered to those who would escape the political storms of their time—a counsel echoed by Saint-Beuve a century ago—would today almost certainly arouse the suspicions of the secret police. This not only marks the distance which Europe has come from the absolutisms of yesterday; it is a sign that, except for the leader and his entourage, everyone has lost his private life without acquiring a public one.

In democratic countries like England and America— democratic because the leadership is still largely responsible to representative bodies, and subject to vigorous criticism by rank and file citizens—the area and power of executive authority have been enormously expanded. This is in part a consequence of the trend toward state capitalism in their economies; in part a consequence of the necessity of total defense in the struggle for survival against totalitarian aggression. But whatever the reason, the facts are unmistakable and are becoming plainer and plainer every day. With the possible exception of the field of foreign policy, the discretionary powers of the American President and the British Cabinet Ministers in the last few years surpass anything dreamed of by their democratic forebears.

Where so few can apparently decide so much, it is not

surprising that interest in the historical significance of outstanding individuals should be strong. It does not require theoretical sophistication to realize that everyone has a practical stake of the most concrete kind in whatever leadership exists. Personal views and virtues in the political high command may spell public disaster or welfare. For once, at least, Mr. Everyman's moral appraisal of those in high places—if only he can keep it above the plane of village gossip—has historical relevance and justification.

The fundamental logic of the situation, to which we shall often recur, that gives intelligent point to contemporary interest in our theme, is this: Either the main line of historical action and social development is literally inescapable or it is not. If it is, any existing leadership is a completely subsidiary element in determining the main historical pattern of today and tomorrow. If it is not inescapable, the question almost asks itself: to what extent is the character of a given leadership causally and, since men are involved, morally responsible for our historical position and future? As we shall see, those who do speak of the inescapability of a specific historical future either belie their words by their actions as well as by other words, or else they compound their belief in an inescapable future with another one in the inescapability of a certain specific leadership, usually their own, which will lead us to this future. Sometimes they do both. We also shall see that to deny the inescapability of the main line of historical action does not *necessarily* mean that what it *will* be always depends upon the character of the leadership. There are more things in history than "laws of destiny" and "great men." As far as the historical role of leadership is concerned, it is a question of degree and types of situation. Our task will be to indicate roughly to what degrees and in what types of situation, it is legitimate to say that leadership does redetermine the historical trends by which it is confronted, and in what type of situations it is legitimate to say that it does not.

2. Another source of interest in the hero is to be found in the attitudes developed in the course of educating the young. The history of every nation is represented to its youth in terms of the exploits of great individuals—mythical or real. In some ancient cultures the hero was glorified as the father of a nation, like Abraham by the Israelites, or as the founder of a state, like Romulus by the Romans. Among modern cultures the heroic content of historical education in the early years has remained comparatively unaffected by changing pedagogical fashions. This may be due to the dramatic effect of the story form that naturally grows up when history is treated as a succession of personal adventures. Or perhaps it reflects the simplest approach to the moralistic understanding of the child. Reinforced by folklore and legend, this variety of early education leaves a permanent impress upon the plastic minds of the young. To ascend from the individual to social institutions and relations between individuals is to go from the picturesque and concrete to an abstraction. Without adequate training the transition is not always easy. This undoubt-

edly accounts for the tendency of many people to personify "social forces," "economic laws," and "styles of culture." These abstractions compel and decree and rule, face and conquer obstacles almost like the heroes of old. Behind the metaphor in much orthodox Marxist writing one can almost see "the forces of production" straining at the shackles with which Capital and Profit have fettered them while human beings, when they are not tugging on one side or another, watch with bated breath for the outcome.

Even on higher levels of instruction the "heroic" approach to history has not been abandoned. The school of American historians who clustered around James Harvey Robinson and the "New History" has given an impressively realistic account of the American past. But in imagining that they were dispensing with heroes and great men to follow the sober course of economic and social "forces," they were deceiving themselves. They removed the kings, statesmen, and generals from their niches and then set up in their places the great captains of industry and finance, and the great thinkers in philosophy and science. The substitution is undoubtedly an improvement but its implication is difficult to square with their theory of the historical process which systematically underplays the significance of the individual. The intelligent student often gets the impression from their work that, for example, "Rockefeller, Gould and Morgan were the truly great men of the era; if they had only been utilized in the political field *how different things would have been!*" [1]

[1] This quotation is from a student's paper.

In our own day, this attitude toward the hero and leader is not merely the unintended by-product of historical education. In most countries, particularly totalitarian countries, the cult of the hero and leader is sedulously developed for adults as well as for children and students. Here again technical advances in communication, together with the new psychological methods of inducing belief, make it possible to create mass enthusiasm and worship of leaders which surpass anything evolved in Byzantium. Where a Roman emperor was able to erect a statue of himself, modern dictators can post a million lithographs. Every medium is exploited by them to contribute to their build-up. History is rewritten so as to leave no doubt that it was either the work of heroes, predecessors of the leader, or the work of villains, prototypes of the leader's enemies. From the moment the leader comes to power, his activity is publicly trumpeted as the proximate cause of every positive achievement. If crops are good, he receives more credit for them than does the weather. Similarly, the historical situation which preceded his advent to power is presented as a consequence not of social and economic causes but of a conspiracy and betrayal by the wicked.

Today, more than ever before, *belief* in "the hero" is a synthetic product. Whoever controls the microphones and printing presses can make or unmake belief overnight. If greatness be defined in terms of popular acclaim, as some hasty writers have suggested, then it may be thrust upon the modern dictator. But if it is not thrust upon him, he can easily arrange for it. It would, however, be a serious error to assume that the individual who affects history—that is, who helps redetermine the direction of historical events—must get himself believed in or acclaimed, as a condition of his historical effectiveness. Neither Peter the Great nor Frederick II had a mass following. It is only in modern times, where populations are literate, and lip allegiance to the democratic ethos prevails even in countries where its political forms are flouted, that the leader must get himself believed in to enhance his effectiveness. It should also be noted that the modern leader or dictator has emerged in a period of mass movements. In consequence he must have a mass base of support and belief as a counterweight to other mass movements. Mass belief in him before he reaches power is born of despair out of need, and nurtured by unlimited promises. Once he takes the reins, the dictator needs some mass support to consolidate his power. After that he can manufacture popular belief in his divinely ordained or historically determined mission almost at will.

Mass acclaim, which was not a necessary condition of the leader's effectiveness in past eras, is not a sufficient condition of historical effectiveness in the present. A figurehead like the King of Italy or a royal romantic like Edward VIII may be very popular, but he decides nothing. For our purpose the apotheosis of an historical figure is relevant only when it permits him to do historically significant things which he would have been unable to accomplish were he unpopular or without a mass following.

3. Whoever saves us is a hero; and in the exigencies of political action men are always looking for someone to save them. A sharp crisis in social and political affairs —when something must be done and done quickly—naturally intensifies interest in the hero. No matter what one's political complexion, hope for the resolution of a crisis is always bound up with hope for the appearance of strong or intelligent leadership to cope with difficulties and perils. The more urgent the crisis, the more intense is the longing, whether it be a silent prayer or public exhortation, for the proper man to master it. He may be called "savior," "man on horseback," "prophet," "social engineer," "beloved disciple," "scientific revolutionist," depending upon the vocabulary of the creed or party. Programs are important, but they are apt to be forgotten in periods of heightened tension, when want or danger is so palpable that it sits on everybody's doorstep. Besides, programs are only declarations of intent and promise. As declarations, they remain in the limbo of the possible until they are realized, and for this competent leadership is required. As promises, they can be betrayed or broken, depending upon who makes them and who carries them out.

Despite their theoretical pronouncements, according to which every individual, no matter what his status, is a chip on a historical wave, social determinists of all hues cannot write history without recognizing that at least *some* individuals, at *some* critical moments, play a decisive role in redirecting the historical wave. Engels speaks of Marx, Trotsky of Lenin, Russian officialdom of Stalin in a manner completely at variance with their professed ideology. Even theological determinists like the Popes, who believe we can trace the finger of God in all historical events, speak of western culture since the Reformation as if it had been created by Luther and Calvin behind God's back. The twists and turns by which these contradictions are extenuated we shall examine later. The fact remains that, for all their talk of the inevitable, the determinists never resign themselves to the inevitable when it is not to their liking. Their words, however, confuse their actions both to themselves and to others. In the end we understand them truly by watching their hands, not their lips.

Crises in human affairs differ in magnitude and intensity. But, judging by the history of peoples of whom we have more than fragmentary records, there has never been a period which has not been regarded by some of its contemporaries as critical. History itself may not inappropriately be described as one crisis after another. Whatever the social forces and conditions at work, and they always are at work—*insofar as alternatives of action are open, or even conceived to be open*—a need will be felt for a hero to initiate, organize, and lead. The need is more often felt than clearly articulated, and more often articulated than gratified. Indeed, the more frequent the cries, and the higher their pitch mounts for an historical savior or for intelligent leadership, the more *prima facie* evidence accumulates that the candidates for this exalted office are unsatisfactory.

A democratic society has its "heroes" and "great men,"

too. It is no more exempt from sharp political crisis than other societies, and rarely lacks candidates for the heroic role. It selects them, however, on the basis of its own criteria. Where a democracy is wise, it will wholeheartedly co-operate with its leaders and at the same time be suspicious of the powers delegated to them—a difficult task but one which must be solved if democracy is not to become, as often in the past, a school for tyrants.

4. The role of the great man in history is not only a practical problem but one of the most fascinating theoretical questions of historical analysis. Ever since Carlyle, a century ago, proclaimed in his *Heroes and Hero-Worship* that, "Universal History, the history of what man has accomplished in this world, is at bottom the History of the Great Men who have worked here," the problem has intrigued historians, social theorists, and philosophers. Unfortunately, Carlyle's book was not taken for what it is—a tract for the times, full of damply explosive moral fervor, lit up here and there with a flash of insight, but contradictory, exaggerated, and impressionistic. Instead it was taken as a seriously reasoned defense of the thesis *that all factors in history, save great men*, were inconsequential. Literally construed, Carlyle's notions of historical causation are clearly false, and where not false, opaque and mystical. Some of his apostrophes to the great man and what is permitted him apologists could use for any totalitarian leader to throw a mantle of divine sanction around his despotic acts—if only they are sufficiently ruthless and successful. On the other hand, Carlyle's paens to revolution could be cited in justification

by any man who fires at a king or dictator—and doesn't miss.

The Spencerians, the Hegelians, and the Marxists of every political persuasion—to mention only the most important schools of thought that have considered the problem—had a field day with Carlylean formulations. But in repudiating his extravagance, these critics substituted another doctrine which was just as extravagant although stated in language more prosaic and dull. Great men were interpreted as colorful nodes and points on the curve of social evolution to which no tangents could be drawn. What is more significant, they overlooked a possible position which was not merely an intermediate one between two oversimplified contraries, but which sought to apply one of Darwin's key concepts to the problem; namely, *variation*. According to this view, the great men were thrown up by "chance" in the processes of natural variation while the social environment served as a selective agency in providing them with the opportunities to get their work done.

It was William James, the American pragmatist, who took up the cudgels for a position which had been rendered unpopular among historians and the reading public by the scientific high priests of social evolution. Controversial zest together with a lack of interest in specific problems of economic and historical causation led him to a disproportionate emphasis on the role of the individual. But he formulated his position in such a way that it was free from the Carlylean fantasy that the great man was responsible for the very conditions of his emergence and effectiveness. James's thesis sounds extreme enough; yet in stressing "the receptivities of the moment" which must be met before greatness becomes actual—receptivities that leave a Leonard Nelson in obscurity but carry a Hitler to the summits of power—he goes far in mitigating its severity. His recognition of the relative autonomy of the realms of nature, society, and individual personality, combined with his belief in the plurality of historical causes, carries to the heart of the problem. And this despite the fact that these views were derived from a larger philosophical attitude about the place of man in the world and not from a study of specific historical issues.

Nonetheless, James's thesis as he left it is oversimplified and invalid. "The mutations of societies from generation to generation," he tells us, "are in the main due directly or indirectly to the acts or examples of individuals whose genius was so adapted to the receptivities of the moment, or whose accidental position of authority was so critical that they became ferments, initiators of movement, setters of precedent or fashion, centers of corruption, or destroyers of other persons whose gifts, had they had free play, would have led society in another direction." [1]

What William James is saying is that no significant social change has ever come about which is not the work of great men, and that the "receptivities" of today which make that work possible are the result of the acts or examples of the outstanding individuals of yesterday. This

"Great Men and Their Environment," in *Selected Papers on Philosophy*, p. 174, Everyman Edition.

may seem to cover adequately the vast changes that have unrolled before our eyes as a result of Lenin's effort to reorganize the world along new social lines. It may, perhaps, throw some light from a new direction on the efforts of Hitler and Mussolini to conquer and enslave Europe in order to prevent not only Lenin's plan from being realized but any democratic transformation of European society. Yet the First World War, and the breakdown of Russian economy which gave Lenin his chance, were certainly not the result of the act or example of any great individual. Nor were most of the antecedent conditions of social conflict—political, economic, ethnical—that were set off in 1914 attributable to the acts or examples of an individual.

The rise of capitalism, the industrial revolution, the march of the barbarians from the east, the Renaissance—none, of course, would have been possible without the acts or examples of individuals. But no matter what *particular* individuals are named in connection with these movements, there is no evidence that the individuals were indispensable in the sense that without them these movements would not have got under way.

The easy contention that, had a "great man" been present, the First World War, say, would never have taken place cannot be upheld by any empirical evidence so far known. He would have had to be a very special sort of "great man"—that is, of a sort that has never appeared in comparable situations. Not infrequently contentions that make much of the decisive influence a great man would exercise if only he had been there are in

principle not verifiable.[1] This is the case when the hypothetical great man who would have prevented the First
World War is identified not in virtue of independent
traits but in terms of his hypothetical success. This is
tantamount to offering a definition of what would constitute a great man in these circumstances. Our point
here is not that the First World War was inevitable, but
that the presence of a "great man" on the order of the
great men of the past would probably not have altered
matters much. Some other events could have altered
things to a point of preventing the occurrence of the
war, nor do we have to go to the realm of natural catastrophes to find them. For example, had the international
socialist movement lived up to its pledges made at the
Basle Congress, war might have been declared but it
could not have been fought. But as far as the particular
problem is concerned, no matter what *individuals* had
occupied the chancellories of Europe in 1914, the historical upshot of commercial rivalries, Germany's challenge to British sea power, chauvinist resentments in
western Europe, the seething kettle of Balkan intrigue,
would very probably have been much the same.

Fashions of interpretation have shuttled back and
forth between historians and philosophers of history during the last hundred years. On the one hand we have
sweeping forms of social determinism according to
which the great man is a symbol, an index, an expression,
an instrument or a consequence of historical laws. To be
sure, distinguishing traits between a great man and other

[1] This is not true of all "If" questions. See Chapter Seven.

men are recognized. But as a forceful writer of this school has put it, "The 'distinguishing traits' of a person are merely individual scratches made by a higher law of (social) development." On the other hand, we have the conception of the possibility of perpetual transformation of history by innovators whose existence, strategic position, and shattering effect upon their fellow men cannot ever be derived from the constellation of social forces of their day. Intermediate views have not been wanting. They have expressed little more than the eclectic belief that sometimes the great man and sometimes the weight of environment controls the direction of historical change. But they have not specified the general conditions under which these factors acquire determining significance.

Once the theoretical question is firmly grasped, no one interested in understanding history can escape formulating some answer to it. There has hardly been a great period or outstanding individual in history that has not been handled differently by historians with varying attitudes toward the question. During the twentieth century the overwhelming majority of historians have been in unconscious thralldom to one or another variety of social determinism. This has not prevented them from conducting fruitful investigation. Much light has been thrown on the fabric of social life of past times and on the slow accumulation of social tensions which discharge themselves with volcanic fury during periods of revolution. Without impugning the validity of their findings, one wonders whether they have done as much justice to the activity of the leading personalities during the critical periods of world history whose roots they have uncovered so well. Too many figures of history have been surrendered for exploitation to *belle-lettrists* and professional biographers who draw their subjects with one literal eye on earlier portraits and one imaginative eye on Hollywood.

5. The psychological sources of interest in great men may, with as much justification, be regarded as means by which great men exert influence on their followers. These sources are, briefly, (a) the need for psychological security, (b) the tendency to seek compensation for personal and material limitations, and (c) the flight from responsibility which expresses itself sometimes in a grasping for simple solutions and sometimes in a surrender of political interest to professional politicians. These sources are obviously interrelated, but for purposes of analysis we shall treat them separately.

a. The fact that the great man or leader often thinks of himself as the "father" of his country, party, or cause, and is even more often regarded by his following as their "father," may seem to lend color to the Freudian view that most individuals are in perpetual quest of the father (or mother) who supplied the axis of security and emotional stability in their early youth. There is a certain insight expressed here which, as is the case with whatever of value has emanated from Freud and his school, is completely independent of the mythological underpinnings of the Freudian system. Many people never outgrow their dependence on their parents, teachers,

or whoever it is that plays the dominant role in sup-
plying their wants, quieting their fears, and answering
their questions as they grow up. Consequently, there is
always ready a pattern of belief and acceptance, of in-
cipient behavioral adjustment, that may be filled by a
leader who talks and acts with the assurance of a parent
and makes claims to a role in the community analagous
to the role of the father in the family.

The more troubled the times and the more conven-
tional the education, the stronger are the vestigial patterns of dependence, and the easier it is for the leader to
slip into its frame. Whether or not the latter proves himself by works is a minor matter at first. To adapt a re-
mark of Santayana: for those who believe, the substance
of things hoped for becomes the evidence of things not
seen. The leader cannot, of course, survive irresistible
evidence of catastrophe, but he is under no necessity to
enhance the material security of those who believe in
him because the belief itself, at the beginning, eases their
fears and increases their confidence.

It must not be overlooked that the psychological need
for security is inconstant both in existence and intensity.
When the need is present, social contexts and pressures
rather than raw, instinctive impulse determine what emotional shelters are sought. During times that are relatively untroubled, and particularly where education
makes for critical maturity instead of fixing the infantile
response of unquestioning obedience, the need for a
father-substitute is correspondingly weakened. Under
other historic circumstances where great leaders and in-

dividuals do not appear, an institution like the Church or *the* Party will assume the primary role of authority.

b. Perhaps a more important source of appeal made by the leader to his following lies in the vicarious gratification of their yearnings through his presumed traits and achievements. The splendor, the power, the flame of the leader are shared imaginatively. New elements of meaning enter the lives of those who are emotionally impoverished. The everyday disparities and injustices of social life, and sometimes the lacks and incapacities of personal life, fade out of the center of concern. The ego is enlarged without effort and without cost. The skillful leader makes effective use of this, especially in the modern era of nationalism when fetishistic attitudes toward abstractions like the state and nation have been developed. By identifying his struggle for power with these abstractions, the leader effects a transference to himself of emotions previously directed to historic traditions, institutions, symbols, and ideologies. He is then able to change the old and established in the name of the old and established.

The tendency to compensate for one's deficiencies by sinking them in the glorious achievements of more fortunate mortals may be an ever-present feature of social life. It may even explain, as Ludwig Feuerbach persuasively argued, the character of the gods men worship. But it should not be lost sight of that the persons and traits chosen for identification are historically variable. There usually are at least two possible ideals into which a need may be projected. A poor man may worship a rich god or an austere one; a people suffering from injustice may exalt a just ruler but they may also take pride in the fact that their tyrant is greater than all other tyrants. Why individuals should feel glorified in the exploits of a Hitler rather than in the wisdom of a Goethe, in the ruthlessness of a Stalin rather than the saintliness of a Tolstoy, cannot be explained simply in terms of the tendency to seek vicarious satisfaction for their limitations. The type of satisfaction sought is derived from the values of their culture.

c. If everyone, or even many, were candidates for political leadership, social life would be far more disturbed than it is. We would not need to be fearful of this disturbance if mechanisms of selection were evolved that would give us highly qualified leaders responsive to the needs and wishes of an informed and politically active electorate. But this is a long way off, and we are discussing what has been and is. A survey of political history shows that aspirants for leadership constitute, comparatively speaking, a mere handful in every community. The truth seems to be that the overwhelming majority of people have little desire to assume positions of power and responsibility.[1]

Conditions of political leadership, of course, change, but politics pursued as a professional career has been and always will be a risky game. Sometimes reluctance to serve as political leader has been so strong that elections have been conducted by lot as in the Greek cities. Even

[1] *Cf.* the remarks of Robert Michels in *Political Parties*, Eng. trans., pp. 49 *ff.* New York, 1915.

in modern times individuals have often been "drafted" from plow or workshop or office to fill offices. The point is, not that there is ever really lacking a sufficient number of persons willing, and even eager, to assume leadership, but rather that the ease with which such persons usually acquire and keep power, and the manifold ways by which they expand the authority originally delegated to them, would be impossible unless there were comparatively so few others interested in competing for the posts of leadership. So long as they are permitted to grumble, most people are gratefully relieved to find someone to do their chores, whether they are household chores or political chores. Politics is a messy business, and life is short. We put up with a great many evils in order to avoid the trouble of abolishing them.

This feeling is natural even if it is not wise. Political leadership is a full-time career with little opportunity for relaxation or cultivation of other interests. In retrospect few intelligent men who have enjoyed power have felt that its rewards were commensurate with the personal sacrifices it entailed. According to one of Plato's myths, Odysseus, the crafty politician, chooses as his lot in his next reincarnation on earth a humble life in a forgotten corner far from the alarms of politics. What is true for the successful politician is also true for his rival. Serious political *opposition* is likewise a full-time activity. In political struggle, therefore, the integrated individual who has a plurality of interests, which he is loath to sacrifice on the sullied altars of politics, is always at a disadvantage. So is the sensitive and high-minded idealist who shrinks from the awful responsibility of deciding, quite literally, other people's lives, and from the moral compromises and occasional ruthlessness required even by statemanship of a high order. Further, political questions are difficult. We accept a great many decisions because we have not the dogmatic certitude that we know what decision is the right one, although we do know that some decision is necessary.

Yet it is an old story that when we refuse to upset our "normal life" by plunging into the political maelstrom, and entrust power to others, we awake someday to find that those to whom we entrusted it are well on their way to destroying "the normal life" we feared to interrupt. This is not only an old story but an ever-recurrent one. It will repeat itself until it is widely realized that political decisions must be made in any event; that responsibilities cannot be avoided by inaction or escape, for these have consequences; and that, considered even in its lowest terms, political effort and its attendant risks and troubles are a form of social insurance.

To the extent that knowledge of these elementary truths spreads and is acted upon, interest in political leadership becomes critical. Identification with it is then a conscious process, not a quest for a father-substitute. We may legitimately take credit for its achievements to which we would not be entitled if it were the work of our fathers, for whom we are in no way responsible. To the extent that these elementary truths are disregarded, every aspirant to leadership—even to dictatorship—can count to an appreciable degree upon the indifference of the population. They will yield him homage after he has succeeded. Whether they do or don't, if *he* cares enough about it, he has the means today to make them pay homage to him.

We have briefly considered several of the sources of interest in the work of the "great man." There are undoubtedly others. We have stressed only those which indicate the existence of the general problem of his influence and limitations as well as its contemporary importance. So far we have been using the terms "hero" and "great man" in the large and unprecise sense in which they are employed in common parlance. We shall find that many different things are understood by these terms and that we shall have to work out an adequate definition for our purposes as we go along. All senses of the term "hero," as used by the adherents of heroic interpretations of history, presuppose that whatever the hero is, he is marked off in a qualitatively unique way from other men in the sphere of his activity and, further, that the record of accomplishment in any field is the history of the deeds and thoughts of heroes. It is necessary to look a little more closely at these premises.

II *The Heroes of Thought*

Aʟʟ ᴍᴇɴ belong to the same biological species, but the differences between them are so marked that they extend to their very fingertips. These differences are more than skin deep. They can be observed in human behavior long before corresponding differences, if any, are discovered in organic structure. The significance of variation, to which these and other facts testify, has not yet been intelligently reflected in our educational and social practice. On the one hand, superficial physical differences have been inflated into differentia of mythical racial divisions in the interests of inequitable social organization. On the other hand, potentially significant differences in personality have been lost sight of in programs of uniform training. But however we evaluate the differences between men, the existence of these differences, natural and acquired, cannot be denied. When it is denied, it turns out that only the *relevance* of certain differences to some particular problem or need is being denied.

Many variations between men are reducible to differences in quantitative degree, for example, height, weight, physical strength. No man is so strong that he cannot be overcome by a group of individually weaker men. If men made history only by virtue of their physical strength, the strong men of our time would be national heroes instead of vaudeville attractions.

But other kinds of variation between men show not only great disparity but irreducibility. Genius is not the result of compounding talent. How many battalions are the equivalent of a Napoleon? [1] How many minor poets will give us a Shakespeare? How many run of the mine scientists will do the work of an Einstein? Questions of this kind are asked not to get an answer but to bring home the uniqueness of genius.

It is not enough, however, for those who believe in the importance of outstanding individuals in history to establish the fact of the *existence* of outstanding individuals. They must present the evidence that these individuals not only existed but had a decisive influence on their respective fields of activity. Further, they must be able to meet reasonably the challenge that if these individuals had not lived and worked as they did, their work would, in all likelihood, have been done by others.

At first glance the position seems to be quite easily established. Particularly in the arts and sciences, evidence pouring in from all sides makes it abundantly clear that the original patterns are created by a few great individ-

[1] Napoleon probably had himself in mind when he said: "An army of rabbits commanded by a lion is better than an army of lions commanded by a rabbit."

uals and imitated by the merely talented many. A casual survey of some of the major cultural fields makes this plain. In what follows we shall present this survey as it might be made by a protagonist of a modified form of heroic determinism.

The titanic figures who dominate the history of literature and drama, include Aeschylus, Sophocles, Euripides, Lucretius, Virgil, Dante, Shakespeare, Milton, Goethe, Balzac, Dickens, Dostoevski, Tolstoy, Proust, and Joyce. Other names may be added to this incomplete list, as well as to other incomplete lists in kindred fields. But whoever adds them will insist upon two things: that they are roughly of the same stature as the writers enumerated, and that there is a vast dimensional difference between them and the tens of thousands of poets, dramatists, and novelists whose minor excellences we enjoy without feeling the breath of greatness in their works. It matters little that no two lists will be identical. If we run the lists up to a hundred of the greatest individuals in the literature of western civilization, we need but select the names that are common to all the lists. No one will seriously gainsay the palpable differences between the few figures that appear on *every* list and the multitude of those who appear on *no* list. Nor is the point affected by the observation that great figures in literature, as in other fields, often emerge in clusters. Certain periods in history are undoubtedly more receptive to genius, that is, more stimulating or more sensitive, than others. They make it possible for genius to thrive as well as for more pedestrian spirits. But they do not produce these geniuses any more than a fertile plot of soil, on which both precious flowers and common weeds flourish, can be regarded as the creative source of the flowers.

Inexpugnable differences in taste enter into all surveys of outstanding creation in every field. Shakespeare will be evaluated differently in the eighteenth and twentieth centuries. But if we are interested in the question of influence rather than of "intrinsic" achievement, a more objective consensus may be obtained. By comparing the list of the most influential individuals with the previous list, in which the compilation is made on grounds other than influence, we can determine the extent to which the great figures have also been the most influential. We will find that almost every influential figure appears on the first list, but that many on the first list do not appear on the second. In other words, some great figures may be passed by or ignored by their immediate times and recognized subsequently as isolated peaks of eminence, much appreciated but little imitated. ·

In music, the record of achievement is even more noticeably the record of new forms and their consummate fulfillment, new points of departure and their masterful development, at the hands of a comparative few of all who have made music. Our list of musicians would include Bach, Gluck, Haydn, Mozart, Beethoven, Berlioz, Liszt, Wagner, Moussorgsky, Debussy, Strauss, Schoenberg, Hindemith, and a few others for whom music historians may make out a case. The themes of the music and sometimes its treatment may be accounted for by the tastes of the public or patron whom the musician, like other artists, sought to please. But just as often, the musician chose to please himself. In any event, his virtuosity and originality cannot be explained in terms of pressures and inducements that were common for all musicians of his period.

In literature and music there has been far greater evidence of collective creation—the epic, the chant, the ballad—than in painting, even when we allow for the factories of some of the great masters. And where technical assistance has been rendered, as in some large canvasses and murals, it is completely subordinated to the plan and judgment of the responsible painter. If we compose our list of the most influential figures in modern painting, it will include Giotto, Masaccio, van Eyck, Michaelangelo, Raphael, Titian, Correggio, Rubens, Poussin, Velasquez, Watteau, David, Monet, Cezanne, Van Gogh, Picasso.[1] This is not to say that we can understand the history of painting without taking note of many things outside of painting, ranging from politics to physics. The significant thing about such influences, where they are *relevant*, is what the artist did with them. Materials and techniques, varying with different periods, may have provided common limiting conditions, class and personal associations may have furnished the ideals and allegiances determining the selection of themes, but what marks the unique achievement of the great artist

---

[1] I am indebted to Professor Meyer Schapiro for suggesting some of the names on this list. In compiling the list of the most influential musicians I am indebted to conversations with Professor Martin Bernstein and Mr. B. H. Haggin for some of the names mentioned. None of them, of course, is responsible for the position which these lists are used to illustrate.

is his individual craftsmanship, his sensibility, insight, and power to make us see things in a fresh light.

It is often alleged that in painting, as in music and literature, the great artist meets the need or atmosphere of his time which, in a sense, speaks through him even when he is unconscious of it or in revolt against it. Even if this were true the great artist would prove himself in how he meets that need, not merely in being a creature of it. But it is not always true. Very often the great creator runs counter to the modes of feeling and understanding around him. He has to rely upon his own work ultimately to generate the taste and sensibility which are capable of appreciating his intent and the skill of his execution. One need but read the excommunications pronounced by shocked critics against new departures in the history of art and music to realize to what an extent public taste is gradually transformed by those who have begun by outraging it.

The history of philosophy reflects the history of politics, religion, and science, but no one can make it intelligible without making central in his account the ideas of Socrates, Plato, Aristotle, Plotinus, Aquinas, Descartes, Spinoza, Leibnitz, Locke, Berkeley, Hume, Kant, and Hegel, to stop with the early nineteenth century. Sociological interpretations of philosophy have been unduly neglected, but what they explain is why certain ideas have been *accepted* within a particular milieu, not why they have been *generated*. The influential philosophies which succeed in getting themselves institutionalized are far fewer than the total number projected.

Sometimes ideas that make little headway in their own times, outside the narrow confines of a school, are revived in subsequent periods and used as a leverage to bulwark social power or pry it loose from entrenched positions. If such occasions never arise, these ideas remain enshrined in the great works of philosophy and are sources of perennial interest to lonely and questing spirits in every climate of opinion. Despite the local idiom and emphasis with which they are clothed, certain recurrent themes concerning human life, struggle, and death have a universal appeal to reflective minds in all developed civilizations.

Even when a philosophy lends itself to acceptance, no one has been able to show that its particular system of ideas is *uniquely* necessitated by the needs of the society, or the dominant class within the society, which adopts it. Some other cognate philosophical systems are theoretically just as serviceable. But among all the possible systems that may be exploited for purposes of social idealization or criticism, those that win the competition for acceptance are usually distinguished by comprehensiveness, rigor, practical relevance, and flexibility—virtues that are unequally distributed among philosophers.

What does the history of science show? The cumulative character of scientific discovery, the unity of its method of inquiry, the common problems that are set for it by previous investigators, and the intimate relations between science, industry, and war seem to make extremely unplausible the hypothesis that scientific development owes most of its achievements to the activities of its leading figures. In addition, it is now a commonplace that many epoch-making discoveries in science have been the work of two men working independently of each other, for example, Newton and Leibnitz on the differential calculus, Darwin and Wallace on evolution, Adams and Leverrier on the pertubations of the orbit of Uranus which led to the discovery of Neptune. Grant, too, that a revolutionary discovery may depend upon the contribution of a humble laboratory assistant operating a calculating machine.

Nonetheless, what all these considerations boil down to is recognition of the fact that greatness in science consists in successfully *meeting* theoretical and practical problems rather than in *creating* them, and that science like every other human discipline receives some of its stimuli of development from the needs and pressures of social life. But this does not gainsay a fact, just as obvious, that in order to do the work of a Newton or a Darwin an individual must equal them in intellectual stature. In the absence of a dozen laboratory assistants, it is not mystical to assume that someone else would have been found to turn the crank of the calculating machine or to plot a star map. In the absence of both Newton and Leibnitz or of any comparable intelligence with the power to master their problem successfully (where the power is independently determined), it *is* mystical to assume that some other individual would *necessarily* have been born to do their work. Modern physics owes more to Copernicus, Galileo, Kepler, Newton, Huygens, Lagrange, Laplace, Faraday, Fourier, Clerk-Maxwell,

Hertz, Gibbs, Planck, Einstein, and a small cluster of other luminaries than it does to modern industry and war. It may even be argued that industry and war owe more to the researches of the scientists than vice versa. Indeed, for some of the greatest scientific discoveries, for instance, the theory of relativity, it is hard to establish any plausible connection with problems of industry and war.

Nevertheless, intellectual tradition, social need, and the organization of the scientific community have a far greater influence on the discoveries of scientists than upon the creations of artists and literary men. In the latter fields the production of a new creation with a distinctive form and style is obviously the work of the individual in the sense that, for all his dependence on his culture, it would be absurd to believe that his work would have been given to the world by someone else if the individual artist or writer had not lived. Raphael's Sistine Madonna without Raphael, Beethoven's sonatas and symphonies without Beethoven, are inconceivable. In science, on the other hand, it is quite probable that most of the achievements of any given scientist would have been attained by other individuals working in the field.

But the degree of probability varies with the accomplishment. It is extremely difficult to see how we would go about establishing a legitimate claim that, if this or that discovery had not been made, its subsequent discovery would be unlikely. Yet certain general considerations apply. If Newton had not made his discoveries in mechanics and optics, we can readily believe that others might have done so not long after, for interest in the problems of these fields was widespread and other attempts at their solution by first-rate minds had been independently made. But some other branches of mathematics and physics show creative work along certain lines by an individual who had no outstanding predecessors in the field and from whom all subsequent investigation in the same direction stems. For example, we have no specific evidence that would warrant the judgment that Cantor's theory of transfinite numbers and Einstein's special theory of relativity would have been developed by others. Although it would be rash to assert that no one but Cantor and Einstein would have propounded these theories, the assertion that others would have done so has even less ground. These cases seem to be intermediate between situations illustrated by the discovery of a new chemical element, after the Periodic Table had been set up, and those exemplified by the composition of the *Missa Solemnis.*

The same general pattern of creative activity will be disclosed in almost every field of creation. There are some exceptions, notably religion. This seems surprising since the majority of the great religious movements have derived not only their existence but even their names from their founders—Zoroaster, Buddha, Confucius, Christ, Mani, Mohammed, Luther, Calvin. Yet it would be rash to regard this fact as decisive or even of much weight. The significant things about a religious movement are its social effects and the reasons why it *con-*

tinues in existence, and not the proclamation of a religious faith by a presumed founder. We say "presumed" founder because critical scholarship raises doubts about the actual historicity of some of the founders of ancient religions. And since their teachings were sometimes set down by followers who lived at a later period, we have no reliable way of knowing to what extent the doctrines were faithfully transcribed or altered in the process of interpretation. But even if the fact of their historicity were vindicated, this would have little bearing upon the profound changes in practice and belief which the religious movements associated with their names have undergone. The early church fathers would have been burned as heretics in thirteenth-century European Christendom.

If we judge the origins of past religious movements in terms of the same forces that give rise to religious movements in our own time, we must conclude that, in the main, these movements create their own leaders, who become the dramatic symbols of the needs and aspirations of their following. The moral ideals, as distinct from the theological trappings, which constitute part of religious faith are an ever-present element in the social tradition. In times of acute crisis and of the failure of nerve which marks a shift from attempts at control to quests for salvation, these ideals are coupled with a profound hope that things are really better than they seem. Hope fortified with supernatural belief is the substance of religious faith. The religious leader crystallizes around himself and his way of life a sentiment that is already in existence when he calls unto the faithful. Very few of the masses who respond come under his personal influence. The force of example, especially at second and third hand, usually moves only those whose position of need and desire already predisposes them in its direction.

*   *   *   *

With the exceptions indicated, let us for the moment grant the claims made by the protagonist of heroic determinism in the fields of culture already considered. We may even leave uncontested far more exaggerated claims. The truth is that all the evidence is grandly irrelevant to the theory we are examining save on one extreme assumption which has never been seriously defended. This assumption is that the towering figures of literature, music, painting, philosophy, and science have also been the decisive figures in world history—political, social, and economic. Or, in modified form, this assumption holds that the consequences of the work of a Shakespeare, a Bach, a Raphael, a Newton, a Kant, or a Balzac have been among the major influences shaping the development of society, particularly in the spheres of politics, economics, and social organization.

To attribute such causal significance to the geniuses of the class listed borders on fantasy, except for the men of science, where the suggestion is further from fantasy but hardly closer to fact. Although it is indisputably true that the world of technology has been profoundly affected by the discoveries of "the heroes of science," it must first be established that the major political, social, and historical changes are functions of technological development. Without denying in the least the pervasive influence of first steam and then power on our everyday life and its problems, it still remains true that new tools and techniques implement social policy rather than determine it. The tank and the plane revolutionized modern warfare just as they could have revolutionized our agriculture and transportation system had they been applied with comparable energy in these fields. But it would be foolish to say that they caused Fascism or the Second World War. To be sure, a technological advance may be followed over night by widespread unemployment and want, but the more relevant, if less immediate, cause of that unemployment is a system of social production which makes the continued labor of these men, even if it would be serviceable to the community, unprofitable to those who employ them. Modern workers know better than their forebears, who tried to destroy the machines instead of subjecting them to social control.

Technical innovations do not eliminate alternatives of choice and action. They may narrow the alternatives by ruling out some possibilities; they may be employed to carry out a decision once the alternative is chosen. They do not cause wars or peace, social revolutions—or even changes of ministry. Finally, it must not be overlooked that among the roster of the great names of science are individuals whose scientific theories have had no important technological consequences. The history of technology, compared to the history of pure science, from which it can be distinguished (but not separated) is a history of lesser men, of Fords and Edisons who achieve their prominence because they score first in a race in which so many men compete that no one man seems indispensable for finishing the race. Someone nearly always wins.

The issue before us is located in a different field in which the arts and sciences play a subordinate role. The question is whether the vast political, social, and economic changes which mark off historical periods, or whether the events that are turning points in historical development, are ever attributable to the work of uniquely gifted or uniquely situated personalities. If there are such uniquely gifted or outstanding personalities, what conjuncture of circumstances must arise before they can exercise their influence? Or are they able to play their parts at any time? Detailed inquiries of a specific kind along these lines are rare, but some have been made. We shall presently turn to the most patient and thoroughgoing of them. The problem here is much more difficult than in the fields already canvassed, for all sorts of considerations are confused in defining the "historical hero" as distinct from the heroes of the arts and sciences. Evaluations of historical significance are much more troubled by controversial passions. Robert Ingersoll and H. G. Wells refuse to regard Napoleon as a hero because they do not approve of him.[1] There is

[1] Typical of this attitude is H. G. Wells's characterization of Napoleon.

"Failing (a noble imagination) Napoleon could do no more than strut upon this great mountain of opportunity like a cockerel on

certainly room in history for moral judgments, but they do not enter in determining the actual effects of any individual on human affairs. We may abominate Hitler precisely because we believe that he has revolutionized the civilization of the twentieth century.

In due course, we shall meet the problem of definition head on. But we must first examine the findings of the chief empirical account devoted to the influence of outstanding personalities in history. The account is interesting not only because it tells us that individuals of a certain class make history but *how much* history they make. This brings us to the work of F. A. Wood.

---

a dunghill. The figure he makes in history is one of almost incredible self-conceit, of vanity, greed, and cunning, of callous contempt and disregard of all who trusted him, and of a grandiose aping of Caesar, Alexander, and Charlemagne which would be purely comic if it were not caked over with human blood." *The Outline of History*, pp.898-899, Star edition, New York, 1929.

III *The Influence of Monarchs*

Perhaps the most extreme proponent of the heroic interpretation of history, next to Carlyle, is an American scholar, Frederick Adams Wood, whose contributions have been comparatively neglected in the literature of the subject. What distinguishes Wood from Carlyle and all other followers of the dour Scotch prophet is his attempt to give an *empirical* grounding of his thesis that will withstand critical, scientific scrutiny. Wood's empirical investigations are independent of his rather bizarre "gametic" interpretation of history as well as of his *a priori* construction of the rise of ancient dynasties. His work in general exhibits a curious mixture of shrewd insight, patient inventory, and wild exaggeration. It has its humorous side in his constant reiteration of freedom from bias, although in places he argues for his thesis like a lawyer defending a client, as in his declaration of an objectivity so entire that "it makes no assumption whatever, unless it be an assumption that a book is a book and a printed word is a printed word." [1]

Wood's procedure is very interesting, and an understanding of it is necessary in order to evaluate his findings. He has made a detailed study of 386 sovereigns in western Europe from the eleventh century until the time of the French Revolution. These sovereigns are drawn from the national histories of fourteen countries: France, England, Portugal, The Netherlands, Russia, Prussia, Sweden, Austria, Denmark, Scotland, Turkey, Castile, Aragon, United Spain. The period of world history covered by this survey is one in which monarchs as a group exercised more absolute power, as far as the data on hand indicate, than at any period before or since. At the same time, Wood strikes a balance of the conditions prevailing in the country during the time of each monarch's reign. He then compares the personal qualities and characteristics of the rulers with the condition of their countries in order to determine whether there is any positive correlation between them. Rulers are classified into three groups—strong, weak, and mediocre, designated respectively by the signs "+," "—," "±." The conditions of their realms are likewise classified in three ways, as exhibiting a state of prosperity, a state of decline, or no clear indication of either. These, too, are designated respectively by the signs of "+," "—," "±."

Characterizations of the ruler which determine the group in which he is classified are derived from a comprehensive survey of "standard" historical accounts, en-

[1] *The Influence of Monarchs*, p. 3, New York, 1913.

cyclopedias, and other reference works independently of the point of view from which they have been written. It is in terms predominantly of intellectual traits, not moral ones, that the classifications into superior, "+," inferior "—," or mediocre "±" are made. Wood finds an impressive unanimity in the judgments of historians of varying schools concerning a monarch's "brilliance," "dullness," "intelligence," "stupidity," "military and political capacity" in contradistinction to their judgments of the monarch's "goodness" or "wickedness," or whether he was a boon or curse to mankind.

The condition of a country is judged only in relation to its material history, consisting almost entirely of "political and economic affairs." More specifically, the classification of material conditions as progressive, declining, or as neither one nor the other is made on the basis of historians' statements on the following topics: "finances, army, navy, commerce, agriculture, manufacture, public building, territorial changes, condition of law and order, general condition of the people as a whole, growth and decline of political liberty, and the diplomatic position of the nation, or its prestige when viewed internationally. No attempt is made to include literary, educational, scientific, or artistic activities." [1] Presumably this last is omitted because of excessive relativity of estimates in authoritative histories, but Wood offers no evidence that the relativity of judgment is greater here than it is about material affairs.

The conclusion Wood reaches at the end of this pa-

[1] *Ibid.*, p. 10.

tient procedure is very striking. Comparing the tables of monarchs and the tables of the conditions of their realms, he asserts that their coefficient of correlation is "about .60 to .70 with a probable error of about .05." His most conservative estimate, generously counting all border-line cases against his own hypothesis, is .60 for the value of the correlation coefficient. In terms of percentages, he states his conclusion as follows: "Strong, mediocre, and weak monarchs are associated with strong, mediocre and weak periods respectively in about 70 percent of the cases. Strong monarchs are associated with weak periods, and weak monarchs (including non-royal regents) with strong periods in about 10 percent of the cases. In about 20 percent of the cases mediocre monarchs are associated with strong or with weak periods, or mediocre periods are associated with strong or with weak monarchs." [1]

These correlation coefficients and percentages are extremely high and cannot with plausibility be interpreted as merely coincidental. As they stand, they may be interpreted as evidence of three different hypotheses: (1) that historical conditions have produced strong, weak, or mediocre monarchs; (2) that the latter have exercised the decisive influence on historical condition; and (3) that both monarchs and conditions are the result of some third set of factors. Wood rejects the first and third hypotheses for the second—his own. He asserts, in a statement as moderate as any that can be found in his writings, that "monarchs have influenced history; more-

[1] *Ibid.*, p. 246.

over that monarchs have influenced European history from the eleventh to the nineteenth century very much, and that the characteristics of monarchs are correlated with the conditions of their countries to at least probably $r = .60$."[1]

This thesis is certainly in line with the heroic interpretation of history, but it is tied up in Wood's writings with two other positions from which it should be differentiated, preliminary to any criticism. The first is that the historical hero is primarily the monarch. The second is that the monarch is essentially a biological rather than a social creation. Indeed, Wood rides his biological fancy to the point of referring to royalty as a "sub-variety of the human race."[2]

Wood systematically disregards the influence of eminent nonroyal personages in history even when they serve as regents or powerful ministers of state. He does not deny the superiority of a Richelieu to a Louis XIII or, were he to carry his study into the nineteenth century, of a Bismarck to a Wilhelm I. He counts that monarch weak who permits the reins of power to be taken from his hands by statesman, mistress, or priest. Were we to add these influential nonroyal figures to Wood's list of heroic monarchs, assuming that we take his list on its face value, the claim of the heroic interpretation would be strengthened. And were we to reject his list and his conclusion about the role of monarchs, this would not be a sufficient reply to the more broadly

[1] *Ibid.*, p. 35.
[2] *Ibid.*, p. 275.

conceived heroic theory which counts its heroes in what ever social strata it finds them. It is difficult to understand, except in terms of his obsession with gametic predetermination, why Wood did not extend his investigations in order to determine the correlation between the characteristics of *all* individuals in decisive positions of power for whom data is available and the state of their country.

This gametic interpretation leads him to a blanket disregard of environmental factors and an almost exclusive stress on alleged facts of heredity. According to Wood, "mental qualities are inherited in the same way and to the same degree as physical," and among the mental qualities are all the characteristics, like intelligence, military valor, ambition, whose presence or absence signify the strong or weak monarch. "While the separation into cruel or non-cruel types, licentious and chaste, ambitious and indolent, etc., is not clearly and absolutely defined, the tendency to segregation which is observed is to be expected from the usual workings of heredity." [1] Wood consequently affirms that "modern royalty (from A.D. 1000 onward) as a whole has been decidedly superior to the average European in capacity; and we may say without danger of refutation, that the royal breed, considered as a unit, is superior to any other one family; be it that of noble or commoner." [2]

Concerning Wood's gametic interpretation of history, it is not too harsh to say that his biological theory is at

[1] *Ibid.,* p. 270.
[2] *Op. cit.,* p. 257.

fault, the reasoning from it crude and *a priori*, and the concrete evidence cited inadequate. Whatever reasons there are for believing in the hereditary transmission of mental traits, they certainly do not include the traits which Wood enumerates in classifying his monarchs. Opening his summary tables at random, note his characterization of Joseph II of Austria: "Restless, brave, ambitious, mentally alert and well informed . . . impractical, visionary, incompetent general . . . benevolent, generous, anxious to bring about reforms. Austere but amiable. Praised for his domestic virtues. His chief vice was duplicity." Or this of the Russian Demetrius: "Ambitious, courageous, accomplished, versatile but imprudent. Good-natured, affable, well-meaning. Magnificent." Or this of King John of England: "Not lacking in cleverness or spasmodic energy but devoid of judgment and breadth of insight. Utterly depraved, mean, vindictive, licentious, cruel and false."

There is not a shadow of justification in biological theory for asserting that most of these traits are genetically predetermined. A man's energy may depend upon his native biological endowments, but what makes him "restless" or "ambitious," zealous in war or in study, emphatically does not. Sexual power may be rooted in inherited glands, but it is the height of absurdity to regard "chastity," that is, marital fidelity, or "licentiousness," that is, the pursuit of other people's wives—which is the way Wood uses these terms—as glandular predispositions. There is no reason to assume that St. Augustine's glands changed when he abandoned his concubines for the church and a life of celibacy.

Even about the moot question of "intelligence" Wood is no more persuasive. For, in the main, the sign of intelligence for him is success—"intelligence means the practical acquisition of wealth and power." He infers its inherent presence or absence only from the success or failure in *acquiring* power. The inference might be legitimate if the *opportunities* to acquire power as between monarch and monarch, and monarch and commoner, were the same. But Wood does not venture to assert this except for the misty period of prehistory, concerning which Hegel once remarked that we can be most certain of what we know least about.

In evaluating the comparative significance of heredity and environment in developing the traits of monarchs and in generating the opportunities for the exercise of these traits, Wood resolutely plays down environmental influence. He even denies that monarchs have had better opportunities to develop their talents than have commoners, asserting that whatever superior advantages they enjoyed have been more than compensated for by greater disadvantages. Among the reasons he offers for his conclusion that royal eminence is a gift of nature rather than of society is that monarchs as a class have had greater success in government than their ministers. ". . . the total number of statesmen alleged to be great is less than the total number of monarchs. Opportunity may have [!] helped the monarchs more than the ministers, but as differences of opportunity are shown by other tests to be usually of slight causative value [!], it is not at all likely that such differences would account for the vast differences in the numerical ratios—differences that make it thousands of times more likely than among average people that the breed of kings will produce a statesman." [1]

When one recalls that Wood is discussing a period in which absolute monarchy and hereditary succession were the rule, his statement that opportunity "may have" helped monarchs more than ministers seems a jest, and his reference to the comparative chances of the common people, a snobbish jest. With the same logic one can argue that the reason a hereditary priesthood shows the capacities it does in temple rites is to be found in its genetic superiority to laymen. And so far is it from being a settled thing that "differences of opportunity are shown by other tests to be usually of slight causative value," one can cite numerous tests, ranging from educational to military achievement, which prove that differences of opportunity are often of great causative value. The greatest generals, as is well known, have almost always been professionally trained.

Perhaps the most conclusive evidence that Wood is riding a biological hobbyhorse can be found in his own historical data as well as in the history of monarchy in the nineteenth and twentieth centuries. By his own admission, from the year 1603 to 1811, no sovereign of outstanding capacity, with the possible exception of William III, sat on the English throne. And yet this prolonged

[1] *Ibid.*, p. 261.

period, according to him, was one of continuous progress. The same situation obtains for Scotland. There is no gametic explanation offered for this startling difference between English and Scotch history and that of other European nations. In the entire nineteenth century, monarchs were dwarfed by national statesmen in almost every country. In the twentieth century they were either thrown into the discard or became decorative symbols. Napoleon, a commoner by virtue of gametic and social station, played ducks and drakes with the crowned heads of Europe. A century later, Lenin, Trotsky, Mussolini, Hitler, Ataturk, Metaxes, and other midget followers of the pattern set by the dictators either buried their monarchs or converted the seed of "the most superior" family in the world into paltry retainers. So much for the gametic interpretation of history!

*   *   *   *

The way is now clear for a consideration of Wood's positive findings freed from the quaint conceits of his social Darwinism. Even if we accept his evaluations of monarchs and conditions and the coefficient of correlation between them, this would not be sufficient of itself to establish the view that "the work of the world has been initiated and directed by a few very great men." The correlation suggests as much the causative influence of environment on great men as vice versa—a possibility that Wood dismisses by invalid and question-begging arguments. More important still, the relative value of the correlation cannot be ascertained until we know what correlation exists between national conditions and other variables like technological inventions, climatic changes, discoveries of new lands and resources, and additional factors not immediately dependent upon the decision of monarchs. Theoretically, the coefficients of correlation between these series may be higher than .60. We might be able to make more accurate predictions about the character of a culture on the basis of these series than on the basis of the hereditary constitution of rulers.

If we turn to Wood's specific correlations, our first criticism is that they are between terms too broad to be very illuminating in evaluating heroic action in history. "The state of a country" at any time, or even over a period of time, is too inclusive and indeterminate to assign it to the consequences of individual action. Our own experience of the effects of human actions shows that we regard specific acts of omission or commission as historical causal agencies only when we can link them through a *sequence of events* to some particular happenings and their ensuing consequences. This failure to consider events in sequences vitiates Wood's entire approach, for he has no way of handling eventful action and eventful men in history. For example, if a monarch is a strong character (+) but his reign is chaotic (−), Wood counts this as evidence that he played no decisive role in history. But obviously, the chaotic conditions of his reign may be the result of that monarch's act, some victory or disaster or fateful policy whose consequences we can trace through a sequence of events to the given conditions. Similarly, if a monarch is strong and his country is prosperous, Wood assumes that this is evidence for the heroic interpretation. But such an assumption is gratuitous unless it can be shown that the prosperity of the country (however that be defined or measured) is the result of some historical event of which the monarch, or some other great individual, was the moving soul.

As great a deficiency in Wood's approach is the assumption of causal connection between the contemporary monarch and his reign. What legitimate ground is there for the assumption that the "prosperous conditions" of a country or its "decline" *must* be the result of the characteristics or decisions of the reigning monarch? The state of a country in a specific important respect may be the result of the actions of a preceding monarch in launching a policy whose consequences, for good or evil, unrolled themselves after he disappeared from the historical scene. Louis XV and Louis XVI of France (1731-1793) were "weak" kings, and their eras were marked by miserable social and economic conditions; but these latter may more plausibly be attributed to the activities and policies of Louis XIV (1661-1715), a "strong" king, whose reign was comparatively more prosperous than those of his descendants. The consequences of the industrial revolution in Great Britain were much more pervasive and manifest in the time of Queen Victoria than in the time of George III. Yet it would be absurd to credit her, or Disraeli or Gladstone, with the effloresence of trade and commercial prosperity and their attendant circumstances. Nor, and this is a weighty consideration against all heroic interpretations, is there any justification for attributing the industrial revolution to George III or any contemporary of the period in which it got started. The tremendous revolutionary impact of urbanization on modern culture, to mention only one of the consequences of the industrial revolution, would have taken place no matter what crowned heads and ministerial figures had flourished at the time.

Examining Wood's synoptic tables from another standpoint, we find that the term "prosperity" is too inclusive, even if taken in a "materialistic" sense, to enable us to characterize a period with sufficient definiteness. For Wood the prosperity of a country is inferred from the composite statements of historians concerning its "finances, army, navy, commerce, agriculture, manufacture, public building, territorial changes, condition of law and order, general condition of the people as a whole, growth and decline of political liberty, and the diplomatic position of the nation, or its prestige when viewed internationally." He does not indicate clearly whether a nation must show progress in one, most, or all of these respects to be classified as prosperous. He does not evaluate the relative weight of advances in different fields although he is aware of the fact that a nation rarely "progresses" all along the line. Is a period of great public building, stable conditions of law and order, but excessive taxation and decline of political liberty to be regarded as "prosperous" or not? Or take the actual combination of features adduced by Wood for the England of Charles I. "Expansion of commerce and general material prosperity. Decline in international prestige. Public discontent. Distress during civil war. Parliament struggled for its existence." [1] By what principles does Wood strike a balance of "prosperity" (+) from this array? The question becomes particularly pertinent when we contrast this conclusion with his characterization of the period from 1199 to 1216 in England as "±," that is, as neither prosperous nor in decline, on the basis of the following account. "Turbulence and discord resulting in the Magna Charta. The rights of individuals defined and enhanced. This constitutional growth must be regarded as of great importance." The growth of constitutional democracy in England is indeed of great importance for that nation's subsequent development. Why, then, does it not outweigh the temporary disorders and the local maladjustments of the time?

Periods of violent transformation of the *status quo*, no matter how progressive their ultimate fruits have been, would show relative declines in most of the respects listed on Wood's scale. It is clear that unexpressed value judgments from which the author imagines himself totally free have played a large part in his use of the classifications. This is inescapable when we approach the subject with such inclusive categories as "prosperity" and "decline" and do not break them down into terms designating more limited social phenomena.

In justice to Wood it should be emphasized that he is aware of some of the difficulties, although he does not

[1] *Ibid.*, p. 401.

take them seriously enough. He admits at the outset of
his study to some perplexity concerning the relative
evaluation of political liberty because "one frequently
finds that under strong kings the country flourished in
almost every way except that the people were op-
pressed." He cuts the Gordian knot by treating political
freedom in states like courage and perseverance in individuals, as "middling attributes," partly material and
partly spiritual. He suggests that we "halve" them. This
means either that we make our estimates of the condition of a country independently of the presence or absence of political liberty, or that sometimes, under
conditions not indicated, we should regard freedom from
oppression as essential to a prosperous community, and
sometimes not. In either case, the procedure seems arbitrary. In practice Wood shows that he cannot do without reference to the state of political liberty and at the
same time that he does not know what to do with it. Since
he relies on the historians' *general* appraisals of different
periods, it should be observed that the weight assigned to
political freedom by historians obviously has varied with
their standpoint and philosophy of history. A Mommsen
will view a period differently from a Gibbon, a Taine
will shrink with horror from the political events that a
Michelet applauds. When their judgments are incorpo-
rated into a presumably objective over-all description
of an era, it masks a value judgment.

Nor is it always apparent why Wood classifies his
monarchs as superior, mediocre, and inferior. For his
classifications to have any scientific value, the traits that

determine a monarch's particular class must be independent of estimates of the conditions of his reign, since Wood believes that the conditions are in the main consequences of those traits. To infer the monarch's traits from the conditions of the country, and then to cite these traits as causal determinants of the conditions, would be gross question-begging. And yet one cannot escape the impression that, if the monarchs classified by Wood had lived in different periods, he would have classified their "innate" qualities differently. Of Charles I of England Wood says that his chief faults were "duplicity and obstinacy." Others might say, on the basis of the same data, that Charles I was "shrewd and principled." Perhaps Wood with a different political and religious bias, or considering the king in relation to a less difficult time, would have agreed. Here, too, moral judgments enter integrally into the total valuation of individual character.

Perhaps the most obvious objection to Wood's thesis is its self-imposed restriction to the period before the French Revolution. The whole nineteenth century lay before him with practically inexhaustible materials on the life and fate of monarchs in all countries. But he does not touch it. The reason is clear. Not even the staunchest legitimist would seriously enter a claim for the monarch as hero either in the nineteenth or twentieth centuries, except for the nonroyal usurper, Napoleon. The *decline* of the influence of monarchs in the last two centuries is something which Wood is totally at a loss to explain. The conditions and events that account for this decline cannot themselves be explained as consequences of the action of monarchs. For according to Wood the hereditary factors were relatively constant.

Concluding our study of Wood's evidence for the historic period to which he restricts it, we are compelled to judge his gallant and interesting effort in behalf of royalty as a failure. His position might have been sounder, though it could not have been so extreme, had he made extended case studies of a score of his outstanding figures in order to trace *specifically* what they contributed to determining the course of empire and the direction of the historical stream. Whatever weight his findings have can be sufficiently accounted for by the fact that since he was studying the era of absolute monarchy, sovereigns would naturally have more power for good or evil than in subsequent periods. *But if it is the nature of the historical era which delimits the sphere of monarchical influence, what determines the transition from one era to another?*

We must now turn to the counterclaims of the social determinists who are confident that they know the answer and have solved the problem.

IV *Social Determinism: Hegel and Spencer*

THE REACTION to the exaggerated "heroism" of Carlyle in the nineteenth century did not deny the existence, and even the necessity, of the hero and heroic action in history. What it maintained was that the events to which such action led were determined by historical laws or by the needs of the period in which the hero appeared. These compelling needs were characterized differently by different philosophers—they were "metaphysical," "ideal," "cultural," "political," "economic." We shall use the term "social" to cover them all. These social forces would summon up when necessary from the deeps of mankind some hero whose "mission" it was to fulfill the historic tasks of the moment. The measure of his greatness consisted in his degree of awareness of what he was called upon to do.

For some philosophers heroes were not at all necessary to get the world's work done. They believed that social needs "work themselves out" through the movements of the masses whose individual components, seen from a distance, could not be distinguished from each other. To them only the masses or classes were heroes. And in the writings of some of their disciples, production figures took the place of the masses.

During the nineteenth century all social determinists had in common the belief that whatever significant consequences seemed to result from the action of a hero could be antecedently inferred from a quite different set of considerations. But the inference was always made *ad hoc,* that is, after the hero's work had been observed.

Even when it was held that *an* individual of a certain heroic stature was a necessary link in a necessary chain of a necessary historical pattern, it was rarely asserted *before* the events in which the hero proved himself that any particular individual fulfilled the specifications. Hegel was confident when he saw Napoleon near Jena that he was beholding "the world soul on horseback." But he was even more convinced that if it had not been Napoleon it would have been someone else who would have carried out the dictates of "the cunning of reason" —and if not on horseback, then on foot.

The expression of dissent to the generic view of heroic determinism was not always a specific reply to the doctrine and its proponents. The Hegelian position, which was the most influential of all social determinisms, had already been crystallized before Carlyle acquired vogue. Hegel himself aimed his doctrines at the eighteenth-century rationalists who explained history in terms of personal psychology and good or bad luck. The Marxist position was presented as a corollary from a comprehensive philosophy of history. And although Spencer edged his criticism with a contemptuous eye on Carlyle (as did Buckle and Taine), there was nothing he wrote which did not flow naturally from his dogmas about the iron laws of social evolution.

It will be instructive to consider in some detail these three variations on the determinist theme in respect to the place of the hero.

For Hegel, as for Oswald Spengler who follows him in this respect, the great man is not the product of material conditions, social or biological, but primarily an expression of "the spirit" of his times or "the soul" of his culture. As a culture develops, certain objective needs arise which fulfill themselves through the subjective decisions of men. Men gratify their errant wishes, carry out their urgent duties, pit their intelligence and courage against the obstacles of nature and society—but all the time they are building something different from what they intend. In the dim light of his understanding, each one weaves a strand in the web of destiny which is the Meaning or Reason of history. The great man is the one who is aware that the Reason of things speaks through his words and deeds. He has historical and divine justification in overriding other individuals, even entire peoples, who remain on the level of everyday understanding.

For Hegel every age gets "the great man" it deserves, but what it deserves depends not on its responsible choice between alternatives but on a predetermined pattern laid up in heaven, existing out of time and yet in some mysterious way pervading events in time. The tasks that confront an age, and to which the great man is called, do not arise from the daily problems of winning bread, peace, and freedom from oppression. They are implicit in the logical notion of man and in the organic necessities of social growth without which men could not become truly men, that is, free men. Hegel was convinced that he *knew* that the Germanic people were destined to become a unified nation and the final carriers of the torch of freedom. He did not base his knowledge, however, on the character of German economic or political history or on the heroic personal qualities of the Austrian Emperor or the King of Prussia, to whom he transferred his allegiance. His knowledge was derived from the dialectical necessity of the logical idea of Freedom which seizes and is seized upon by the great men of action and thought. Similarly Spengler *knows* that each culture will have its Alexander, its Aristides, its Socrates, not because of any empirical evidence but in virtue of a metaphysical insight into the eternal life cycle of the social organism which cannot fulfill "the style of its soul" without men of this type.

On this view the greatness of any individual is apparent only *after* the event, when the consequences of what he has done have become plain and when judgment has become safe. Great men do not make history. They are evoked by "great times." Great times are those transitional periods when mankind rises from one level of freedom and organization to another. The great man, therefore, will always be found, but whether he is found in the purple of royalty or in the beggar's robe is relatively accidental.

In what then does greatness exist for Hegel? In some dim perception, translated ultimately into political action, of what the world order is to be. Great men like Caeser, Alexander, and Napoleon are touched by the divine Reason which seems like madness to their sober contemporaries:

> It was not his [Caesar's] private gain merely but an unconscious impulse that occasioned the accomplishment of that for which the time is ripe. Such are all great historical men—whose own particular aims involve these large issues which are the will of the world-spirit. They may be called Heroes, inasmuch as they have derived their purposes and their vocation, not from the calm, regular course of things, sanctioned by the existing order; but from a concealed fount—one which has not attained to phenomenal, present existence—from that inner Spirit, still hidden beneath the surface, which impinging on the outer world as a shell, bursts it in pieces because it is another kernel than that which belonged to the shell in question. They are men, therefore, who appear to draw the impulse of their life from themselves. . . .

> Such individuals had no consciousness of the general Idea they were unfolding, while prosecuting those aims of theirs; on the contrary, they were practical, political men. But at the same time, they were thinking men, who had an insight into the requirements of the time—*what was ripe for development*. This was the very Truth of their age, for their world; the species next in order, so to speak, and which was already formed in the womb of

time. . . . World historical men—the Heroes of an epoch
—must, therefore, be recognized as its clear-sighted ones;
their deeds, *their* words are the best of that time.[1]

We can now understand why Hegel refuses to allow
ordinary mortals to apply their moral yardsticks to the
work of great men and the chosen nations to whom they
belong. For these Heroes are not responsible for their
ruthless deeds. They are the instruments of the morality
of tomorrow—unhappy instruments discarded by the historical process when their work is done. "Their whole
life is labor and trouble. . . . They die early, like Alexander; they are murdered like Caesar; transported to St.
Helena like Napoleon." This is the price of greatness.
The hero may die or appear to suffer defeat, but "history" will always vindicate him.

But we are not deceived by Hegel's plea. His whole
philosophy is an elaborate attempt to shift moral responsibility from the individual acts of individual men to the
impersonal whole of nature and history. His heroes, he
would have us believe, cannot help themselves. Their
acts are necessitated by the same logic that necessitates
their times. He commits the double blasphemy of asserting whatever is, is right and whatever is, is divinely ordained. The chosen heroic few like the unchosen many
do not initiate anything; they play out roles distributed
in advance. World history would have been the same
even if all the world heroes, *per impossible,* had never
existed.

[1] *Lectures on The Philosophy of History,* Introduction, English
translation by Sibree, p. 30, New York, 1900.

A careful study of the passage cited from Hegel will show, once we strip it of its spiritualism, that it contains all the assumptions common to the different varieties of social determinism.

1. No individual makes history *de novo*. He is always limited by his times and his culture. His energy and intelligence may be unique but what he wants and what he sets himself to do, are rooted in what Hegel calls "objective Mind," and what anthropologists to-day call culture—the superindividual institutions of speech, family, religion, law, art, and science. In a sense his activity must be understood not as the action of an individual versus his environment but as the interactive operation of one aspect of a culture in relation to others. The great man can do only what his culture permits but—and this is crucial—*the culture permits of only one direction of development.* There are no genuine alternatives.

2. There is a difference between what men, even great men, imagine they are doing and the objective meaning or significance of what they do. The meaning of their acts must be understood primarily in terms of historical trends that have begun in the past, embrace the present and point to the future. Moral righteousness before the stern deeds of history is the easy privilege of those who judge events one by one. But it is an illusion of finite perspective.

3. The world-shattering deed or thought which testifies to the presence of greatness is possible only when the culture is prepared or ripe for it. The hero must fit in at a certain stage in social development. Delivery may

be forced, but the child must be ready to enter the world. A heaven-storming Promethean will is doomed to fail unless what it wills is already alive in germ in the conditions of the present. "The laurels of mere willing are dry leaves which have never been green." [1]

4. The great man is therefore an "expression," "a representative," "a symbol," "an instrument" of historical and social forces on whose currents he rides to renown and victory. If we want to grasp the source and reason of his greatness, his biography or purely personal traits are relatively unimportant. It is to the society and culture of his times that we must turn. For these are the fields over which great historical forces sweep in majestic sequences that challenge our understanding. Knowledge and mastery of these historical forces, the aim of "scientific" history and social theory, give man social control and human freedom. Here there is a variant depending upon how the term "scientific" is interpreted, whether empirically or metaphysically.

*   *   *   *

In different language and from different metaphysical premises, Herbert Spencer and the host of popular writers whom he influenced reached similar conclusions. Spencer arrives at his conviction about the historical importance of great men not by an empirical canvass of world history but by a simple deduction from his theory of social evolution. The theory of social evolution assumed that all societies developed in a uniform, gradual,

[1] *Rechtsphilosophie*, Lasson edition, p. 317.

and progressive fashion. If an errant genius or adventurer could send society spinning outside of its determined paths, there could be no expectation of uniformity in development and, even more alarming, no assurance of gradualness. Revolution might rear its head to interrupt the slow cumulative changes of evolution.

Although he was no great reader of historical biography, Spencer was confident that "if you wish to understand these phenomena of social evolution, you will not do it though you should read yourself blind over the biographies of all the great rulers on record, down to Napoleon the Greedy and Frederick the Treacherous." [1] Spencer did not go to the absurd extremes of Buckle who first maintained that kings, generals, statesmen, and their like hampered the development of culture, and then called them "puppets" without any historical significance. Great men, if we were interested in labeling these picturesque figures of the past, abounded in history. But to attribute any epochal event to any individual at any time was to lose oneself in a blind alley of misunderstanding. The scientific historian may note in passing that the individual was the proximate or immediate cause of a decisive happening, but he must go on to an investigation of what produced the individual in question and determined him to act as he did. "Before he [the great man] can remake his society, his society must make him." [2]

[1] *The Study of Sociology*, American edition, p. 37, 1912.
[2] The extent to which Spencer's views have influenced modern social thought on the subject of the great man and his environment can hardly be exaggerated. *Cf.*, for example, "The Great Man versus

Let us dwell for a moment on this sentence of Spencer's. It seems to state a commonplace truth. But, like so much of the language of social and political theory, it is pervaded by an unconscious and, therefore, misleading analogy. Strictly speaking an individual is "made" biologically. Before his social environment and education begin to mould his personality, he must at least exist. We can never separate the individual from the personality he begins to take on shortly after he is born, but we can distinguish between certain powers and capacities that differentiate individuals in the same or similar social environments. We know that individuals subjected to similar environmental conditions sometimes react very differently. The very *impact* of the environment is not always similar, because different individuals may meet it differently. Sometimes an enormous disparity is found in the achievements of those who begin with equal or similar opportunities. It is at least an open question whether this disparity may not be due to the presence

Social Force," by W. F. Ogburn in *Social Forces*, vol. 5 (1926-7), pp. 225 *ff*. Although more attention is paid to the fact of biological variation than in Spencer, the upshot of the position is much the same. "If one wishes to contrast Lincoln as a great man with the social forces of his times, one must remember that Lincoln, the adult man, represents a part of the social forces (since they helped to produce him) with which it is desired to contrast him." "Great men are thus the products of their times, that is, their achievements influence the times. The great man is thus a medium in social change." The study concludes: "The great man and his work appear therefore as only a step in a process, largely dependent upon other factors." There is no admission at any point of the possibility that "the step" may ever redetermine the direction of the process. A false step may kill a man. Why may not a false step or a timely one spell great disaster or victory for a culture?

or absence of certain strong biological capacities, or to something which is not part of the environing culture. But the use of the term "makes" or "produces" in Spencer's account prevents a nicer discrimination between the indissoluble but distinguishable features of original nature and acquired culture in human beings.

Despite his misleading language, Spencer has admitted enough to compel him to come closer to the problem of heroic action in history. Granted that before the great man can remake his society, society must "make" him, whatever that means. This implies at least the possibility that some men *can* remake society. All men are "made" by society, but only a few can "remake" it. More than this the heroic determinist does not require as a fair recognition of a fact and problem. Spencer has to go further. The words with which he pronounced a blithe dismissal of the hero indicate that the hero is a force to be reckoned with—or at any rate that he is not yet explained away. So far all Spencer has told us is that before a Frankenstein monster can kill a man, he must be made by a man. But the man who creates the monster does not create the things the monster takes it into his head to do. We would hardly say that Frankenstein, if slain by the monster, had committed suicide.

Spencer's biological interests did lead him to the perception that a great man might differ from other men in ways not reducible to differences in social opportunity. When he meets the heroic theory head on, he maintains that the great man is a *resultant* of "a long series of complex influences which has produced the race in which he appears and the social state into which that race has slowly grown." On the basis of his theory of the hero as a *resultant*, Spencer proposes that, instead of attributing a decisive event to the great man who seems to have been its immediate occasion, we seek for the ultimate (Spencer's word is "real") explanation in "that aggregate of conditions out of which both he and they have arisen."

Put in its simplest form, Spencer proposes that, instead of explaining the great man in terms of his immediate environment or the environment in terms of the activities of the great man, *both* the great man and his environment should be explained in terms of the total state of the world which preceded them. In one sense this is innocent enough; what the world is at any period is explained by what the world was at a period directly preceding it. But scientifically, it is not very fruitful. As William James showed in his trenchant comments on Spencer, this is comparable to explaining occurrences by God's will. Whether the sparrow falls or flies we can always say it was caused by God's will; and no matter what the historical scene is at any moment, with or without a great man, we can always say that it is a natural outgrowth of what the world was at an antecedent moment.

Insofar as Spencer restricts himself to the field of history, his position begs the question at issue. To make this more apparent let us recast his view in the following way: Let C represent the cultural environment of any heroic figure, P his innate powers and capacities, C^1 the historically preceding cultural environment, and P^1 the ancestral line of the man in question. What Spencer is asserting is (1) that every question about the work or significance of an individual is a question about $C + P$; and (2) that $C + P$ can always be explained by $C^1 + P^1$. The second assertion is a *non sequitur*. $C + P$ may be the consequence of $C^1 + P^1 + X$, where X designates any event which has historical *effects* but neither cultural nor biological causes, like fire, earthquake, plague, or accident. If the causes of the latter be included in what Spencer means by "the aggregate of conditions," then his idea runs foul of James's criticism. All he is saying is that today has grown out of yesterday and that tomorrow will develop out of today. At this juncture Spencer must embrace either a tautology or an absurdity.

It is on the first point that Spencer begs the whole question by ruling out the possibility of genuine *interaction* between personality and culture (C and P or C^1 and P^1). In his earlier formulations he had asserted that great men were made by their cultures and admitted that great men could *remake* culture. But his insistence upon taking the great man and his environment together, not as a problem for analysis, but as a situation to be explained by an earlier situation, likewise unanalyzed, simply by-passes the issue. The issue will not be by-passed. It crops up at every turn in our historical experience.

That strategically placed men are subjected to certain pressures, that they sometimes falter and break under them or ride them out and master them, is undeniable. Whether the leading men or the conjuncture of circumstances are more decisive in explaining some specific event of momentous consequence, is an inescapable question. Was Hitler responsible for the anti-Semitic obsession of German Nazidom, an obsession that hindered not helped the Nazi international program of fraud and conquest, or did the cultural environment and history of Germany make it obligatory upon Hitler to persecute the Jews? [1] Granted, although there is no reason to believe it, that Hitler could not have raised his consuming mania to the level of state policy unless the early apostles of anti-Semitism, Chamberlain, Stocker, and the Austrian Lueger, had preceded him. Still, why were the Jews as a group made the scapegoats, when other groups, actually just as guiltless but politically more active, could have served his cunning purposes even more effectively? Nazism without anti-Semitism is conceivable, though it would be just as abominable as the one we know.

From the fact that we can trace the rise of Nazi belief to social conditions, it does not at all follow that its anti-Semitism arose out of these or other social conditions and not out of the hysterical animosity of Hitler. Most of the adherents of Nazism in Germany began by deprecating its anti-Semitism as incidental and transitory—threatening rhetorical bombast, so they said, to force a

---

[1] According to Mr. James G. Macdonald of the *New York Times* (November 29, 1942), Hitler told him in an interview in the spring of 1933 that he intended "to use anti-Semitism as a means toward world domination." Nonetheless, although Hitler's anti-Semitism was an important factor in arousing world public opinion against him, especially in countries he hoped to neutralize temporarily, he intensified his persecutions of the Jews. Only countries he has subdued by force of arms, excepting his original allies, have "adopted" his anti-Semitic decrees.

capitulation without a struggle. But having bet on Hitler and become his willing hostages after he received power, they ended up by accepting and defending anti-Semitism when Hitler showed himself fanatically intransigent on the Jewish question. A faithful Spencerian would have us believe that *both* Hitler and the persecution of the Jews could have been predicted from the state of German culture in the nineteenth century *and* from Hitler's hereditary antecedents. This is not true and would be irrelevant even if it were true.

Were Spencer writing today, without doubt he would contemptuously add Hitler the Bestial to Napoleon the Greedy and Frederick the Treacherous as another illustration of a ruling figure whose biography explains nothing of the march of events. This follows readily enough from the First Principles of Spencer's Synthetic Philosophy but not from a critical study of historical facts. And it is no more true, in the bald, unqualified way that Spencer holds it, of Napoleon and of Frederick than of Hitler. For example, suppose we want to understand why Napoleon invaded Russia in 1812, an act that, as he later declared, was the greatest error in his life. Or why, when he had reached Vilna, he refused to accept Czar Alexander's offer of peace which would have plugged the last leaks in the Continental blockade. It may be that the history of Europe would have been the same even if Napoleon had kept the peace and saved the army of a half million men he lost in Russia. (A *prima facie* case can easily be made out for an opposite conclusion.) But—and this is the crux of the matter—once it is granted that Napoleon *could* have done other than he did, it is the sheerest dogmatism to rule out in advance the possibility that the key to his decision might be found in the personality of "Napoleon the Wicked." What Spencer and Hegel really believe is that neither Napoleon nor any other figure in history *could* have acted differently in any important respect. This tendency toward historical fatalism, from whose explicit implications they shrink and which they sometimes deny, is at the core of their approach to history. Like all fatalism it cannot be supported by any evidence, but it can be held in the teeth of any evidence marshaled against it. The position is irrefutable because it does not risk anything by venturing specific predictions. It represents the triumph of metaphysics over empirical method in the study of history.

V *Social Determinism: Orthodox Marxism*

THE MOST IMPRESSIVE system of social determinism in our times was developed by orthodox Marxism. Its leading ideas are embodied in the writings of Engels, Plechanov, Kautsky, Lenin, Trotsky, and Bukharin. Whether or not these men were faithful to Marx's own meaning in all major respects is historically unimportant, for it was they who determined the dominant theoretical traditions of the Marxist movement. Our exposition and criticism will not aim at comprehensiveness but will focus on the way in which this philosophy treated the problem of heroic action in history.

The impressiveness of the orthodox Marxist position lay in two features which distinguished it from the Hegelian and Spencerian views. In the latter the doctrine of evolution was a metaphysical principle from which the theory of social determinism was deduced by alleged logical principles. Among the Marxists the theory of determinism was presented as a doctrine that rested foursquare on the solid ground of historical experience. They projected their positions, including the conclusions about the role of great men, on the basis of detailed historical studies. These presumably confirmed their fundamental hypothesis that changes in the mode of economic production, and the clash of group interests resulting therefrom, were the determining factor in human history. Where Hegel was mystical and Spencer eclectic, the Marxists considered themselves scientific and monistic.

It is easy to establish that orthodox Marxism, particularly where it invokes the notions of dialectical necessity and historical inevitability, is shot through with metaphysical elements every whit as questionable as the views it criticized. Nonetheless it remains true that it worked over a vast amount of empirical material and made substantial contributions to our understanding of the historical past and present. For *some* periods of human history, it could legitimately claim ample confirmation for its hypothesis, for example, the decline of feudalism, the great wars of the nineteenth and twentieth centuries, the English, American, French, and February Russian revolutions. As a heuristic principle the theory of historical materialism has proved fruitful even when obviously incomplete. It has been adopted, with modifications, by many influential historians who remained indifferent, when they were not hostile, to the political program of Marxism.

The second feature that accounted for the impressiveness of Marxism was its apparent allowance for the role of great men in history. It denied neither their existence nor historical significance and met criticisms with an "of course great individuals are influential but . . ." that seemed to invite further inquiry. Yet, as we shall see, its concessions were hopelessly at odds with its basic position. Where it paid adequate attention to the work of great historical figures—for instance, its own heroes, Marx and Lenin—its historical monism went by the board. Where it interpreted the historical activity of Alexander, Caesar, Cromwell, Peter the Great, Napoleon, as "expressions" of convergent social pressures or merely as "instruments" of class interest, it often abandoned its scientific approach for the mystical *a priorism* which was part of its Hegelian heritage.

Since Engels is the fount of all orthodox Marxist writing on the subject, we shall begin with a discussion of his views. Among the epigoni none has developed the doctrine in such a way as to add anything fresh in content or emphasis to it except Plechanov and Trotsky. Yielding not an iota of their theoretical piety, they were nonetheless more sensitive than their comrades in arms to the difficulties raised by critics. Plechanov's contributions we shall consider after Engels'; Trotsky's in a subsequent chapter.

According to Engels the domain of history is subject to a "necessity" which manifests itself through the host of contingent events that make up our daily experience. This necessity is at bottom an *economic* necessity—a specific expression of the dialectic necessity which reigns in the cosmic whole. Since history is controlled by an economic necessity, the actions of human beings may work with it or against it. If against it, they are doomed to be ineffectual. Only when they work with it can human actions count. The economic development of society, whose motor impulse is the continuous expansion of forces of production, does not proceed smoothly. It develops in virtue of a ceaseless opposition or conflict between these forces of production on the one hand, and the restricting relations of production or the basic legal forms of ownership, on the other.

Since history is made by men and not by bloodless abstractions, the obstacles that stand in the way of this progressive expansion of productive forces must be cleared by men. The greater the task, the greater is the experienced need for change; the greater the need, the greater is the man who *necessarily* emerges to give leadership to the struggle for change. The great man of thought is he who prepares the minds of men for the revolutionary social changes that, unknown to them, are already on their way. The great man of action is the organizer of the struggle between the classes that stand to gain or lose by revolution. *Who* the great man will be we do not know; that *he will be found* whenever he is needed is certain. What his particular ideas and actions will be we cannot tell; that, no matter what they are, their consequences will help liberate the productive forces and gratify the needs of society for a new system of social relations, is assured. In Engels' own words:

> That a certain particular man, and no other, emerges at a definite time in a given country is naturally a pure chance. But even if we eliminate him there is always a

need for a substitute, and the substitute is found *taut bien que mal;* in the long run he is sure to be found. That Napoleon—this particular Corsican—should have been the military dictator made necessary by the exhausting wars of the French Republic—that was a matter of chance. But in default of a Napoleon, another would have filled his place, that is established by the fact that whenever a man was necessary, he has always been found: Caesar, Augustus, Cromwell. (Letter to Starkenberg.)

The difficulties in this position are so obvious that it is hard to explain its widespread acceptance among those who pride themselves on their allegiance to scientific method. Engels tells us that a great man is a necessary response to a social need for him. But how do we know that there is a social need for him? Surely not after the event! That would be viciously circular. If we can recognize the need for a great man before he appears, then, in the face of the history of wars, revolutions, class struggles, and momentous social problems, it would be no exaggeration to say that there is *always* a need for great men. But where are they? On Engels' assumption that a great man is a necessary response to a social need, he should always be present. History would still be a domain of economic necessity, but the mode of its assertion would always be through great men. Yet Engels admits that great men make their bows only infrequently on the stage of history.

For Engels social need is not only a necessary condition for the appearance of a great man but also sufficient. But how does he know that, even when a great and urgent social need is present, a great man *must* arise to cope with it? Who or what guarantees this blessed event? Not the Providence of Augustine and Bossuet, not the Cunning of Reason of Hegel, not the Unknowable of Spencer, but "the dialectical contradiction between the forces of production and the relations of production."

This dynamic force works in a truly remarkable fashion. But one wonders by what specific chain of causation it guides the union of sperm and egg out of which is generated the individual whose qualities enable him in season to achieve greatness. And how does the dialectical mode of economic production go about finding a substitute for the great man it produces but fails to keep alive? How long must the run be before the substitute is found? What happens to the urgent social need or historical crisis in the meantime? Does it obligingly wait until he turns up? The resolution of economic contradictions is historically necessary, says Engels. The union of sperm and egg is historically *accidental,* he adds. How then does historical necessity get itself translated into the realm of biology? One is tempted to paraphrase Hamlet's exclamation to his father's ghost: "Well done, old metaphysical mole! Cans't work i' the earth so fast? A worthy pioneer!" Or does Engels believe that just anybody can substitute for Caesar, Augustus, and Cromwell?

Test Engels' position by selecting any historical period and answering these questions in concrete terms. Suppose we ask why a great man failed to appear to answer the crying need for the unity of all the anti-Fascist forces in Germany—a unity which probably would have prevented Hitler from taking power save after a violent and prolonged civil war, and which, under certain circumstances, might have resolved the economic distress that gave Hitler his audience and following? Who will deny the need? Who will deny the failure to meet it? Even by way of a substitute! Does the failure of a great man to appear at this time indicate that he was unnecessary or that the victory of Fascism was "inevitable"? If the first, why defeat; if the second, why the opposition to the inevitable? Even those who *now* assert that the victory of Fascism was "inevitable" are compelled to acknowledge that among the reasons for its inevitability was the absence of a leadership great enough to unify the movement of millions against it. Indeed, it requires only a slight twist to picture Hitler, on Engels' theory, as the "great man" produced by dialectical necessity to fill the necessary needs of the hour. Engels might shudder at such a conclusion but he could hardly disown the method by which it was reached without abandoning his own position.

Writing in 1880, William James banteringly asked Herbert Spencer whether he believed that if William Shakespeare had not been born at Stratford-on-Avon on April 26, 1564, the convergence of social and economic forces would have produced him elsewhere; and whether, if Shakespeare had died in infancy, another mother in Stratford-on-Avon would have delivered "a duplicate copy" of him? "Or," he teasingly continues, "might the substitute arise at Stratford-atte-Bowe." Fourteen years later Engels answers all these questions affirmatively for Napoleon and other great historical figures. In principle he answers them affirmatively for Shakespeare, too. The sole qualification he insists on is that the substitute might be a little better or worse rather than an exact replica.

One final word and we may leave Engels dangling on this *reductio ad absurdum* of his position. If "social need" is more narrowly defined, so that it is not true to say that it is present in all historical periods, we may question whether a social need invariably precedes the appearance of a great man. The citizens of Thebes and of the other cities he razed to the ground were not conscious of any social need when Alexander appeared outside their walls. Or the masses may be aware of a social need which the hero may frustrate rather than fulfill. They may want peace or socialism. He may give them war and dictatorship—in the name of their "deeper" needs. They may want long lives and merry ones. He may send them to heaven in droves for the salvation of their souls. And where "a social need" is met by the activity of the outstanding leader may it not sometimes be that the social need is the consequence of his earlier work? It may take a hero to undo his own mischief.

* * * *

George Plechanov was the best oriented philosophical intelligence among the orthodox Marxists of his generation. This tribute was paid to him both by Karl Kautsky and Nicolai Lenin, leaders of the two wings of Marxist orthodoxy. Plechanov discussed the problem of the hero in history in many of his writings. It was a singularly acute question for the Russian Marxists of whom he was the recognized theoretical head. It was acute not merely as a theoretical question but as a practical and political one. The political program and philosophy of the Narodniki—Russian socialist populists—were allegedly based on the view that history could be influenced in significant fashion by great individual protagonists of the word, and even more, of the deed. This group and its popular successor, the Social Revolutionary Party, rejected the Marxist views of determinism and social evolution. Without denying the influence of material factors, social and economic, they placed an even greater emphasis upon personal and ethical decisions in history. They refused to forswear the use of individual terror as a policy of combating oppression. They held strategically placed individuals, not "the system" that bred them, responsible for social evils and political excesses. Both on practical and theoretical grounds, therefore, Plechanov took the field against them. His best treatment of the subject was given in *The Role of the Individual in History*.[1]

In the course of his discussions Plechanov rejects not only the views of the defenders of the heroic interpretation of history but also those of the determinists who, in opposing the former, declared the individual to be a "*quantité négligeable*" in history. Both have dismissed a problem which is of great importance, not merely to Marxism, but to any scientific understanding of history.

[1] Originally published in 1898, English translation, New York, 1940.

Plechanov presents his doctrine as a "synthesis" of the truths contained in two simple conflicting views. He implies that this synthesis is "a full and definite solution of the problem of the role of the individual in history" which Guizot, Mignet, Thierry, Monod and Lamprecht —determinists all—failed to solve. He uses as a foil to his argument some remarks of St. Beuve, who believed that at any given moment a sudden decision of will by a great personality might redetermine the course of history.

We shall use a series of illustrations to test the consistency and adequacy of Plechanov's position, and in order to sharpen the issues, the same series that Plechanov employs.

1. The influence of Madame Pompadour on Louis XV was very profound. The fateful alliance with Austria during the Seven Years' War seems to have been the result of her work. During this war the French generals, particularly Soubise, again and again revealed themselves as hopelessly incompetent. Madame Pompadour protected Soubise with disastrous consequences to the French cause. If she had not waged a needless war on the Continent, France might have preserved her colonies from English encroachments. The failure to throw everything into the defense of her colonial empire was again the work of Madame Pompadour who for personal reasons sought to ingratiate herself with Maria-Theresa by allying the French and Austrian fortunes. The loss of the war and of her best colonies had a definite and important effect, Plechanov admits, on France's subsequent economic development.

2. During the same war, Austrian and Russian troops had surrounded Frederick II, near Striegan. Frederick's position was desperate, and an attack, which could easily have been made, would have annihilated him. But Buturlin, the Russian general, dallied and then withdrew his forces. Frederick was saved and upon Empress Elizabeth's death, a few months later, recouped his fortunes. Of this incident Plechanov says: "It is not improbable that Buturlin's irresolution saved Frederick from a desperate situation. Had Suvorov been in Buturlin's place, the history of Prussia might have taken a different course." That Buturlin should have been the commanding general instead of a man like Suvorov, he admits, is historically accidental. He also concedes that the accidents of the Seven Years' War had a decisive influence on the subsequent history of Prussia, although he asserts that their effects would have been entirely different at a different stage of Prussia's development.

3. During the French Revolution, what would have happened if Mirabeau had not been removed by premature death, and if Robespierre and Napoleon had? As for Mirabeau, the constitutional monarchist party would probably have held power a little longer. But even with Mirabeau it would have been unable to withstand the surge against republicanism. If Robespierre had been killed in 1793, his place would have been taken by another. Whether that person would have been superior or inferior we cannot tell. But we can tell, Plechanov assures us, that "events would have taken *the same course* as they did when Robespierre was alive." And so with

Napoleon. Had he been struck by a bullet, as he almost was, at the siege of Toulon, or died of the scurvy he contracted there, or committed suicide in Paris in 1795 as he planned, nonetheless, "the French Republic would have emerged victorious from the wars it waged at that time, because its soldiers were incomparably the best in Europe." The consequences of the 18th Brumaire would have unrolled even without Napoleon. If Napoleon had not nominated himself to bear "the good sword" which the Abbé Siéyès needed to behead the French Revolution, any number of generals could have wielded it.

The details of Plechanov's historical illustrations as well as the validity of his historical judgments are of subsidiary interest. His method and argument, however, are of the first importance in appreciating the approach of social determinism. Let us examine a little more closely what he does with the historical incidents in question.

1. The defeat of French armies in the reign of Louis XV, Plechanov assures us, should really not be laid at the door of the glamorous Madame Pompadour. Defeat was already prefigured by the military deterioration of the army, its lack of discipline, and its unreliable officer staff, drawn from the decaying remnants of the aristocracy more intent upon pleasure than upon glory. These "general causes," even without Madame Pompadour, would have been "quite sufficient" to ensure a lost war. By playing favorites and keeping the incompetent Soubise in a position of command, this famous lady only made a bad situation worse. Neither she nor anyone else could have saved it.

All this is straightforward enough. Plechanov, however, insists that Madame Pompadour ruled not in her own right and name but through the king, who was docile to her will. But the character of this king obviously did not follow necessarily from the general course of French economic development. Given the very same economic, social, and historical setup, a king of a very different character might have appeared, say a home body and family man, or a misogynist. In either case Madame Pompadour would have been out of the historical picture even if she had remained at court. But if we grant the possibility of there arising a king of a different character, concludes Plechanov, then it follows that "these obscure physiological causes," which produced a lascivious ruler instead of one who was pure of heart or powered with only a mild sex drive, *"by affecting the progress and results of the Seven Years' War, also in consequence affected the subsequent development of France; which would have proceeded differently if the Seven Years' War had not deprived her of a great part of her colonies."* [1]

This is straightforward, too, but in an opposite direction from the position taken previously. Suddenly the military causes previously listed are no longer *sufficient* to ensure defeat. They could have all been present, and yet by grace of another pair of gametes victory might have been snatched from the English, the colonies saved, and the development of France profoundly altered. This smacks more of Wood than of Marx and Engels. Plecha-

[1] *Op. cit.,* p. 39, my italics.

nov is well aware that he has something to explain. "Does not this conclusion," he continues, "contradict the conception of a social development conforming to laws? No, not in the least. The effect of personal peculiarities in the instances we have discussed is undeniable; but no less undeniable is the fact that it could occur only *in the given social conditions.*" [1]

What a comedown from the pretentious thesis that Plechanov in common with other orthodox Marxists had set out to prove! Of course, the influence of any set of personal traits or personal peculiarities is what it is only in given social conditions. *The same would be true if an entirely different set of individual traits were present.* Their influence, too, would be limited by the given social conditions. But the question is whether their influence would have the same or different effects from those of Louis XV's personal traits. In one paragraph, Plechanov says the effects would be the same. In another paragraph, he says the effects would be different. He squares the contradiction in a third paragraph by saying that, same or different, the effects of personal influence would be influenced by social conditions.

Plechanov could have made even a stronger case for the position that the influence of Madame de Pompadour was natural in the French society of her time. She was not the first or the last mistress of Louis XV. Nor was Louis XV the first or the last French king to make a mistress a power at the Court. Indeed, one might say that *maîtresse-en-titre du Roi de France* was a permanent

[1] *Op. cit.* Italics in original.

institution at the French court from the time of Charles IX. Nor did the French bourgeoisie resent an institution which was not unknown to their own circles. They objected only to the expense involved in keeping the favorite and all her relatives, which added to the burdens of taxation, and even more to any favorite who interfered with the administration of state. How natural seemed the relationship between the king and his favorite is evidenced by the fact that Madame de Pompadour was encouraged by her own mother, Madame Poisson, who was definitely of bourgeois origin, to consider herself at quite an early age as the future mistress of the king. Because of her comeliness she was openly spoken of in the family circle as *un morceau du roi*—literally, "a royal morsel" or "a piece for the king." [1] But all this only shows that Louis XV could have been influenced by the ruling mistress but not necessarily by Madame de Pompadour, and not necessarily in the direction in which her tastes ran—tastes that were rather unusually intellectual for her station.[2]

Plechanov's methodological error here is far-reaching

---

[1] See *Mémoires of Madame du Hausset, Waiting Woman of Madame de Pompadour*, translated with an Introduction by F. S. Flint, p. 8, London, 1928.

[2] Plechanov does not altogether do her justice. She was unusual in her line—if she had been less of an intellectual she would have interfered less in matters of state. Besides determining foreign policy, making and unmaking ministers and generals, she broke up the Jesuit order and expelled its members from France—her only popular act—founded the porcelain factory at Sèvres as well as the École Militaire which later trained Napoleon, befriended and protected Voltaire, Montesquieu, Crébillon, Quesnay, her private physician, Diderot and others of similar talent.

and pervades other philosophies of history as well.
Neither Plechanov nor any other historian can plausibly
argue that the complex of social conditions necessitated
in any way the emergence of the personal traits admitted to have "affected the subsequent development of
France." All that can be claimed is that some personal
traits could not have influenced conditions, that the latter exercised a check or veto upon some of the personal
traits of leading historical figures. For example, an idiot
boy would not be permitted to become a ruler, a vio-
lently insane general would not be entrusted with a
command, a militant atheist could never become the
prime minister of a Catholic country, an incurably honest man would never be allowed to fill a diplomatic post
that requires a Talleyrand. But despite this, there remains a whole range of widely different traits that rulers,
statesmen, generals, diplomats, and revolutionary leaders may possess; and different combinations of these
traits might very easily have different historical effects
on the given conditions.

What Plechanov is asserting is comparable to the statement that wheat and a deadly variety of mushroom, as
distinct from stones, owe their effects on the human organism to given physiological conditions. True, for not
everything can influence the body. But among the things
that can, some may nourish it and others may kill it.
Similarly, not all types of individuals can influence given
social conditions, and whoever does so, must meet these
conditions. But once we admit that individuals can influence historical developments, then it is not precluded

that at certain periods different individuals, through their activities and ideas, may give rise to different developments. A modern Ajax would occupy a booth in a side show of a circus; a Joan of Arc, in a scientifically enlightened age, wandering into General Headquarters with a tale about "hearing voices" would be sent to a psychopathological ward for observation. They would not influence events. But, to use Plechanov's own illustrations and admissions, a Suvorov in place of a Buturlin, a Louis XVIII instead of a Louis XV, a concubine more intelligent and less fearful than Madame de Pompadour in respect to foreign policy, might have affected the course of empire.[1]

2. What Plechanov has done is to substitute at this point, before his final relapse into orthodoxy, a quite different theory of history from that held by Engels and other orthodox Marxists. He is *not* affirming that heroes are made by their times. He is *not* predicting that a social need for a great man will produce him. He is *not* denying that great, or even weak, individuals can redetermine the course of history. He is maintaining that the time, place, and extent of the changes wrought by these individuals depend upon the economic conditions of their day, and the interplay of class interests which grow out of these conditions. To this no one but a mysti-

---

[1] It should be remembered that we are not discussing the historic truth of Plechanov's illustrations but only his method. Madame de Pompadour had perhaps less influence on French history than Plechanov believes. At this phase of his thought, *he* must believe that she was, so to speak, a heroine in reverse, instead of just another beautiful, brainy, and ambitious woman.

cal extremist like Carlyle would object, but many historians would add supplementary sets of limiting conditions to the freedom of the great man. This independence of thought on Plechanov's part would be admirable were he aware of it and were he not trying to prove that it was perfectly compatible with doctrinaire economic determinism which denied that there are any genuine alternatives in phases of social development and that, *a fortiori*, individuals cannot at any time be instrumental in deciding between them.

In discussing the fate of Frederick II, Plechanov repeats the general pattern of analysis. Buturlin saved Frederick's neck. Suvorov would have wrung it. But the effects in either case would have depended on the social-economic conditions of Europe. Nonetheless, the admission is clearly made that the history of Prussia would read quite differently if it had been Suvorov instead of Buturlin. That it was Buturlin and not Suvorov is an accident. Therefore, and this is really courageous coming from an orthodox Marxist, "It follows that sometimes the fate of nations depends on accidents, which may be called *accidents of the second degree.*" [1] A historical accident, as Plechanov had the merit of seeing, is not an uncaused event. As Cournot had long before pointed out, it is the point of intersection between two or more series of events which are themselves determined. The point of intersection cannot be predicted from the laws determining any or all of the series. It is clear that whoever takes the role of accident in history

[1] Plechanov, *op. cit.*, p. 42.

seriously cannot be a monist. But orthodox Marxists are monists. Hence we await Plechanov's attempt to wriggle out from the contradiction between his theoretical dogma and his empirical reading of history.

It takes the form of a shift from one question to another. Accidents count—superficially and ultimately. But despite all this, historical determinism as understood by Engels is valid. Why? Because accidents "do not in the least hinder the scientific investigation of history." Granted, although one might wonder whether inability to predict these "accidents" does not hinder in some respect their scientific investigation. Granted, but what has this to do with the issue as between a great variety of historical theories, all of which assume that accidents are no bar to the scientific investigation of history? That issue is: which of the hypotheses associated with the theory of heroic determinism, historical materialism, climatic variation (Huntington), psychological determinism (McDougall, Tarde, Freud), etc., enable us to systematize our existing knowledge of society and history most coherently and to predict most reliably what the course of future historical events will be? Or, to state it differently, granted that the field of history is "subject" to laws: what *kind* of laws, or combination of laws, will enable us to predict historical developments with the degree of accuracy relevant to the subject matter? Plechanov here believes that he has vindicated orthodox Marxism by offering as evidence in its behalf the possibility of scientific investigation. But the possibility of scientific explanation, which is a program for the quest of causes and laws, is neutral as between conflicting scientific explanations that submit themselves to the control of evidence.

3. If the merit of the system of orthodox Marxism is that in the hands of a gifted individual like Plechanov it leads to the turning over of historical material from a new point of view, its defect is that it blocks the proper assessment of what is uncovered. Just as we are getting ready to credit Plechanov with a refreshing willingness to follow the lead of evidence, he relapses into the economic monism which his own discussion of the case studies he submits completely refutes. The reason for this relapse is the mistaking of a hoary methodological fallacy for a valid logical principle, an error that will be found in the writings of every dogmatic monist of any school.

Plechanov points out that considerable opposition existed to Madame Pompadour's maleficent influence but that public opinion could not prevail against her. French society of her day could not enforce its judgment of condemnation. Why? Because of its form of organization which made the monarch immune from the controls that existed in a country like England where the purse strings could be effectively tied even against the royal fingers. But why did this form of organization exist in France? Because it was determined by the relations of social forces. Hence, he concludes, "it is the relation of social forces which, *in the last analysis*, explains the fact that Louis XV's character, and the caprices of his favorite, could have such a deplorable influence on the fate of France."

This may seem plausible enough until one inquires: why was the relation of social forces in France what it was? What determines it? And what determines the cause that determines it? And since we are in quest of "a last analysis," why stop there? It is obvious that this procedure sets up a chain of infinite and irrelevant questions which Plechanov brings to an arbitrary halt when he reaches the relation of social forces. But the relation of social forces has no ascertainable bearing on the specific question of the specific causes and consequences of Madame Pompadour's influence. One might ask whether in fact French society had no means of getting rid of Madame Pompadour, either by the not unknown method of assassination or by the introduction of a rival siren who concerned herself exclusively with the boudoir rather than with politics.[1]

But these are minor matters compared to the main assumption behind Plechanov's argument.

This assumption is that the cause of a cause of a cause of a cause of an event is the cause of that event. To put it concretely: because the mode of economic production is the cause of the existing form of social organization, which is the cause of the failure to compel court

[1] Either method would not have been difficult. Madame du Hausset in her *Mémoires* tells of many threats of assassination against Madame de Pompadour. And she relates a curious confession of her mistress to Madame de Brancas, a confidante, who remonstrated with her over her diet. "I am tormented by the fear of losing the King's heart and ceasing to please him. Men, as you know, set store on certain things; and I have the misfortune to be of a very cold tempera-

favorites to refrain from interfering with affairs of state, which is the cause of Madame Pompadour's refusal to yield to public opinion, which is the cause of deplorable effects on the history of France, it follows, according to Plechanov, that the mode of economic production is the cause of Madame Pompadour's deplorable effects on French history.

This assumption is fallacious because it converts what is at best a necessary condition of the event to be explained into a sufficient cause of the event. Of course, French society had to exist before anyone could influence it. Of course, the state of French society at a given moment had to be what it was before any individual could have the specific effect he had on it at the next moment. But it by no means follows that *because* of the existence and state of French society any particular person had to influence it; or that *because* France had a certain form of organization, the individual who did influence it had to be good or bad, capable or foolish. Plechanov focuses his error in two key sentences. "Why was the fate of France in the hands of a man who totally lacked the ability and desire to serve society? Because such was the form of organization of that society." [1] The "because" is a complete non sequitur.

Plechanov's assumption is fallacious because it over-

---

ment. My idea was to adopt a somewhat heating diet to remedy this defect, and for the last two days this elixir had done me some good, or at least I think it has." *Op. cit.*, p. 52. The heating diet in question consisted of "chocolate flavored with triple essence of vanilla and scented with ambergris, truffles and celery soup."

[1] *Op. cit.* p. 41.

looks what he had previously recognized, namely, that the final event of the series of causes he has built under it may be more relevantly explained by an event from an entirely different series of causes. The biological cause of John Smith's existence is his parents, of his parents, his grandparents, of his grandparents, his great-grandparents. John Smith's election to office is the result of another series of causes, social causes. His elopement with the town secretary stems from still another. Now, unless his great-grandparents had existed, John Smith would not have been born, but it would be taxing them with too much to hold them responsible for his birth although they may explain some of his biological characteristics. Unless he were born, he could not have been elected to office, but his election is more relevantly explained by the political issues of the campaign. Unless he had been elected to office, he might never have encountered the town secretary, but his elopement probably can be satisfactorily explained in terms of what happened after he met her. Plechanov insists upon bringing in the great-grandfather, not only as the cause of John Smith's existence but of his election and elopement, too.

Finally, Plechanov's assumption is fallacious because it implies that there is "a last analysis" or an "ultimate cause" which is always relevant and therefore is independent of a specific question and context. Since Plechanov believes that "the development of productive forces [is] the final and most general cause" of historical events, the duty devolves upon him to show concretely that it is relevant to the event he has set himself to explain. His conscientiousness as an empirical historian often leads him to acknowledge that the proximate, determining causes of an event have nothing to do with the state of productive forces and social relations. His allegiance to a metaphysical dogma then seduces him into *changing the subject under investigation* in order that these forces and relations may be introduced with some show of plausibility. Thereupon they are declared "in the last analysis" to be the "ultimate causes" of the original subject of investigation.

It is unnecessary to follow Plechanov's divagations in detail in his treatment of Napoleon, which follows the same pattern as the examples already considered. Plechanov assures us that what Napoleon achieved on the field of battle would have been won by other generals. Perhaps so; but it is a little hard to swallow in face of the evidence showing that French armies were almost always defeated or immobilized whenever Napoleon entrusted their command to other officers. Even the retreat from Moscow would not have been nearly so disastrous if it had not been for the errors of Murat and Berthier to whom Napoleon left his army when it was a two days' march from Vilna. In order not to embroil himself in these matters, Plechanov professes a certain disinterest in the purely military outcome of Napoleon's campaigns. Even without Napoleon, he tells us, the history of Europe would have been substantially the same because of the inexorable development of productive forces which were bursting through their feudal integuments. This implies that the military victory or defeat of French arms must be regarded as comparatively unimportant in its effect on the social and economic life of France.

The implication, however, cannot be sustained. Plechanov himself admits that the political changes which would have followed upon a successful invasion of France might have influenced its subsequent development to a considerable degree. Surely, the Bourbons and the Church, if restored soon after the 18th Brumaire, would not have reconciled themselves easily to the expropriations and social changes that had acquired the sanction of a generation's use and wont by the time Louis XVIII returned to the throne. To take only one phase of Napoleon's effect on the social and economic life of France, even Engels acknowledged that the Napoleonic laws of inheritance were of tremendous consequence. The abolition of primogeniture and the limitation of the freedom of testamentary disposition resulted in a multiplication of small farm holdings throughout France and to the preponderant influence of the peasantry on French life. This is cited as an illustration of the *reciprocal* influence of law and politics on economic development. There is no reason to assume that the early restoration of Bourbon rule would have led to the adoption of a legal code similar in essentials to the Napoleonic code. The code, together with other achievements of the French Revolution, influenced Europe only after the victory of French arms.

We may assume, therefore, that, for the historic period in question, a military victory was required to permit the free expansion of productive forces in Europe. Was this military victory, then, inevitable? In virtue of what? Of the antecedent state of development of France's productive forces? Or by virtue of Napoleon's military genius? Plechanov does not venture to affirm the former. Were he consistent in his economic monism, he would be compelled to do so. His position reduces itself to the belief that, although France's military victory was necessary for her economic development, Napoleon's military genius was unnecessary for France's military victory.

What, then, accounts for the glorious record of success that blessed French arms? According to Plechanov, "The French Republic would have emerged victorious from the wars it waged at that time because its soldiers were incomparably the best in Europe." [1] Note two things. Plechanov's explanation is military. He does *not* claim that the superiority of the French soldier was the inescapable consequence of the state of French productive forces. Second, the same incomparable French soldiers lost battles when they were commanded by other generals and won them when they were commanded by Napoleon. Something more than legend must account for the almost unanimous judgment of military authorities of all countries that Napoleon was the greatest military genius in modern history.

Despite anything that may be said about Napoleon, Plechanov clings firmly to the belief that like all men of

[1] *Op. cit.,* p. 47.

talent he is "the product of social relations." Talented people can influence only individual features of particular events but not their general trend, for *"they are themselves the product of this trend."* This is true not only in politics, war, and social relations but in art, science, and literature. "Here too," he concludes, "in the last analysis, everything [!] depends upon the course of social development and on the relation of social forces." [1]

Plechanov has come the full circle—despite the heterodox epicycles—from dogma to dogma.

*   *   *   *

Its inadequacies notwithstanding, social determinism has left a permanent deposit on the thought patterns of our time. We must assess the value of this deposit before we can carry our theme forward. It is clear that, as long as scholarship remains free and is not *gleichgeschaltet*, the naïve glorification of the hero as the creator of an age will no longer have any intellectual standing. The hero will always be taken with his time and his problems. But is this all that has been won by social determinism? Or is the heritage of social determinism, purified of its extreme versions, richer and more usable than this?

[1] *Ibid.*, pp. 52-54.

VI *The Framework of Heroic Action*

LOOKING BACKWARD on the claims of the social determinists, whether idealist or materialist, it would appear that all they have validly established as a universal generalization is that a great man cannot influence history until the times are "ripe" for him. This is a far cry from the thesis they set out to defend. For, like ripe fruit that may rot on the vine or be harvested, the times may wither unfulfilled or be plucked by a man of action. So much even Carlyle might have admitted, insisting only that the ripeness of today is the consequence of the heroic action of yesterday.

An arrogant claim tamed down to a commonplace truth, the reader may murmur. Yet it is not altogether a commonplace when we realize that it does more than set definite limitations upon heroic action. It suggests why such action can succeed in meeting the challenge of ripe conditions. This may be clearer if we contrast it with other views of Carlyle.

In some of his moods Carlyle seems to agree with the social determinists that the hero is limited by the kind of world into which he is born. But even here there is a difference. For Carlyle is vague about the nature of the limitations set by the world whereas the historical determinists, at least, are quite specific about the nature of the limitations. They are social, political, and economic.

Corresponding to this vagueness on Carlyle's part is his notion that the capacity of genius is not specific but has, on the contrary, an *unlimited* power of creative adaptation to whatever world it discovers. "Napoleon," says Carlyle, "has words in him which are like Austerlitz battles." And again, "The hero can be prophet, poet, king or priest or what you will according to the kind of world he finds himself born into. I confess I have no notion of a truly great man who could not be *all* sorts of men." [1]

The social determinists usually have a more sober view of the specificity of talent and genius. For them social conditions are not always permissive to genius; they may be crushing. And when they are permissive, there are limits to the range of possibilities of heroic action. These limits can be inferred from the whole complex of social traditions, habits, tools, and techniques, and the clash of group interests. It is this complex of culture traits which, without explaining the existence of genius, throws some light on its historical development and responsiveness to the "ripe" conditions. Carlyle would have held that

[1] *On Heroes, Hero-Worship and the Heroic in History,* Everyman edition, p. 312.

Newton born into a community of Australian primitives would necessarily have made some major scientific discovery and that a Napoleon would have been a great savage military chieftain. Plechanov and other social determinists, on the other hand, realize that man is an "acculturated organism," to employ a favorite expression of John Dewey. He is dependent for his intellectual power not only upon his biological capacities but upon the society that sets the framework of interest and attention within which doubt and inquiry arise, and that supplies the very words which both inspire and limit the ideas that germinate within him. There is no good reason to believe that if a man with the biological endowment of Newton or Raphael or Napoleon had been born in early prehistory he would have rediscovered fire or created magnificent ornaments and paintings or achieved renown as a warrior.

The social determinists left a richer bequest to modern thought than an insight into the multiple ways in which genius is tied to culture. They made us sensitive to the *interrelatedness* of the different expressions of culture although they absurdly overstated the extent of the interrelation. But of greatest importance was their insistence on the notion of determining trends in history which, despite the mystical metaphysics that accompanied it, expressed a certain truth.

Instead of peeling off the metaphysical husks from the doctrine of social determinism in order to discover its kernel of truth, let us restate this truth independently.

All of us are aware that both in nature and history

certain events seem more relevantly connected than others. As soon as they got down to concrete cases, the social determinists, too, acknowledged this. Even if we were to grant that in some sense all events are connected with each other, we would still have to recognize that some are more intimately bound up with one another than others. The living organism is often pointed to as an illustration of an organic system of which all parts are interdependent. Yet the loss of a finger will not necessarily affect vision, though a disease of the optic nerve will. Many of the body's parts and functions may undergo change without noticeably altering the capacity to think. So in the pattern of historical events. We are confident that some of the events antecedent to the present war, like the romantic marriage of Edward VIII, were not causally relevant to its outbreak. No one could plausibly argue that his marriage brought on the Second World War, or that if he had "renounced the woman he loved" and continued as king, it would have been prevented. Endow him with any trait or quality of your favorite hero, and still there would be little ground to believe that he could have forestalled the approaching showdown between Fascist Germany and Democratic England. The latter event, although not literally inevitable, was in the making or "in the cards," to use a colloquialism. There were certain important conflicts of interests between the two sides which seemed to be pressing these countries into war. These conflicts have been observed in the past to lead to wars between nations in western society independently of the character of their sovereigns, and no large-scale war has been observed to occur when such conflicts have been altogether absent. It is historical situations of this type which the social determinists validly stress in discounting the influence of outstanding individuals.

There are other historical situations in which we can legitimately say that, although an individual's act has been part of the pattern of events culminating in a great happening, the event would have occurred without him although not at the same time. For example, as far as its influence on the development of Europe is concerned, Columbus was the first to discover America. We are all cognizant of the intrepidity he displayed and the hardships he underwent during the voyage. Nonetheless, most historians would be ready to admit that, even if his ships had foundered, the new world would have been discovered anyhow. And they would maintain this even if it had not in fact been rediscovered by Amerigo Vespucci. The expanding technological facilities of nascent capitalism, the desire to exploit more intensively the markets of the East, the quest for a short passage to India—Columbus himself died in the belief that he had discovered eastern Asia—made it only a matter of time before the western hemisphere would have been reached by enterprising sailors. The record shows that the whole period was one of enterprise and discovery. Here, then, we can again say that there were "determining" tendencies in the social and economic history of Europe, in contradistinction to the social and economic history of the Indian tribes already living in America, which resulted in the discovery of the new world. The remarkable exploits of a Columbus, a Vespucci, a da Gama, a Magellan were not historically necessary; but *what* they did was. They themselves were colorful incidents in a course of development whose configuration cannot be explained by the activity of particular individuals no matter how gifted. They were not historical heroes in the sense of eventful or event-making figures because they cannot be considered as having been indispensable to the discoveries with which their names are linked.[1]

These "determining tendencies" are not disembodied forces, spectral or physical, that compel events to happen. They are all reducible to the behavior patterns of groups of individual men living under determinate historical conditions and traditions. Their responses to the challenges and threats of their environment are sufficiently similar to enable us to predict how they will act in the face of similar challenges and threats. When we rely on determining tendencies to predict the turn of events over a given period or to justify a judgment about the past, our confidence is based upon the assumption that variations in detail may be disregarded in charting

[1] For the meaning of eventful and event-making, see Chapter Nine. There is another sense of "hero," of course, in which it is perfectly legitimate to speak of Columbus as a hero even if we admit that America would have been discovered had Columbus died in his cradle. Jacob Burckhardt, for example, who grants that Columbus was not indispensable to the discovery of America, writes: "Among the discoverers of distant lands only Columbus is great, but very great, because he staked his life and an enormous will-power on a postulate which brings him into the same rank as that of the greatest philosophers." *Weltgeschichtliche Betrachtungen, Gesamtausgabe*, Bd VII, p. 165.

what will take place or what would have taken place. What the social determinists assert is that the "heroes" of history are *always* variations in detail. This, we have seen, is wrong. But it is of tremendous importance to realize that *sometimes* "heroes" are variations in detail, if only because it may cure us of the illusion that a great man or leader can always save a situation or obviate the accumulated consequences of past folly. One of the tragedies of historical life is that men cannot undo the consequences of an event that could have been left undone. The difficult problem is to discover when the "hero" is historical incident and when he is not.

An American dramatist with genuine philosophical insight once wrote a play called *If Booth Had Missed*. He develops the play in an imaginatively plausible fashion to conclude that if Booth had missed, someone else would not have missed. The dramatist was saying in his own way, not that Lincoln's assassination was inevitable, but that it was symbolic of the fact that the Civil War had hardened the attitudes of the North to a point where no further compromises could be made. There is good historical evidence to warrant this judgment. Against a background of four years of bitter civil strife, no president, even one as different as Lincoln was from Andrew Johnson who tried to carry out Lincoln's policies, could have withstood the desire on the part of the victorious states for harsh, rather than conciliatory, treatment of those whom they regarded as the authors of all their woes. If on the night of the fateful performance Lincoln had taken cold, stayed at home, and survived, it is unlikely that he would have succeeded where Johnson had failed. Had Lincoln died after a fruitless effort to convert the Radical Republicans to the ways of foresight and charity, his stature for posterity would have been cut down to that of Woodrow Wilson. The fate of Wilson indicates that the prestige of leading a war to a successful conclusion is not sufficient to cope with the problems of postwar reconstruction.

It follows from what we have said that heroic action can count decisively only where the historical situation permits of major *alternative* paths of development. The denial by social determinists of the orthodox Marxist school that heroic action can ever have a decisive influence on history is usually a corollary to the doctrine that the existing mode of economic production *uniquely* determines the culture on which it is based. According to them, from a given economic system, one and only one other economic system can develop. And on the basis of the economic system thus developed, one and only one culture—where "culture" designates the noneconomic social institutions—can flourish. Where significant variations in the politics, art, religion, or philosophy are recognized, these must be explained "in the last analysis" in terms of the developmental changes of the economic system moved by its immanent "contradictions." Heroes in such a conception can be found only in the interstices and joints, so to speak, of the social economic process. Their presence is irrelevant to the death and birth of new forms of society.

Proof? As far as great men are concerned, not even

an attempt at proof except in the writings of Plechanov and Leon Trotsky. Plechanov we have already considered. We turn now to Trotsky whose effort, despite its ultimate failure, is a truly remarkable intellectual feat which makes a permanent contribution to the scientific understanding of history. His explicit treatment of the theme will be found in his *History of the Russian Revolution.*

Trotsky's thesis is that the occurrence, development, and climax of the Russian Revolution were inevitable. Since that Revolution was made by men, one of his problems is to investigate the relation between the characters of individuals and the historic process. Naturally it is the character of individuals in strategic situations or positions of leadership and power which is his first concern. He offers to show that the traits of character displayed in crucial historic actions have, so to speak, "been grafted, or more directly imposed, on a person by the mighty force of conditions."

As evidence he presents a brief case study of the personalities of Nicholas II and his queen, and of the way they met the rising tide of revolutionary sentiment which broke over them in February, 1917. Relying upon diaries and memoirs of court attendants, he paints a picture of Nicholas II, confirmed by other analysts, as a weak, silent man, completely immersed in the trivial affairs of the day while his world was openly crumbling into ruins, suspicious of his own ministers, vindictive when crossed, and, although absolute autocrat of the largest state in the world, making an impression of complete helplessness on everyone who came into contact with him.

We then have throwbacks to portraits of Louis XVI and Charles I, likewise absolute monarchs confronted by revolutionary crises. Even allowing for certain elements of exaggeration, Trotsky is able to establish an astonishing similarity in their personality patterns, especially as manifested in their treatment of the events that culminated in the loss of their thrones and lives. There is even a striking similarity between the behavior, words, and attitudes of Marie Antionette and Alexandra Feodorovna. Here we have important characters with great authority acting out historic roles that seem to have been written for them.

" 'He did not know how to wish: that was his chief trait of character,' says a reactionary French historian of Louis. Those words might have been written of Nicholas: neither of them knew how to wish, but both knew how to not wish. But what really could be 'wished' by the last representative of a hopelessly lost historic cause? 'Usually he listened, smiled, and rarely decided upon anything. His first word was usually *No*.' Of whom is that written? Again of Capet. But if this is so, the manners of Nicholas were an absolute plagiarism. They both go toward the abyss 'with the crown pushed down over their eyes.' But would it after all be easier to go to an abyss, which you cannot escape anyway, with your eyes open?" [1]

---

[1] *History of the Russian Revolution*, translated by Max Eastman, vol. I., p. 92, New York, 1932, Publishers: Simon & Shuster.

More persuasively than Plechanov, Trotsky is calling attention to the fact that a historic personality cannot be explained from the point of view of the individual psychologist alone, that his traits, intellectual and moral, are products of a continuous interaction between his native powers and social conditions. Does that mean that any king or czar in the place of Louis XVI or Nicholas II would have had the same personal traits? Trotsky is not so rash as to affirm this. He admits that if the historical accidents of heredity had been different, the Russian Revolution might have run into "a very different make of Czar." But the historical outcome would have been the same. The autocracy would have fallen anyway. A strong czar could not have saved it for long.

This shifts the position to the familiar view that the significance of personality in history is limited to comparatively unimportant variations, and that every *major* development in the historical process is determined by social and economic forces in which heroes and great men are a negligible factor. The greater the historic event, the more intense the discharge of accumulated social tensions—the more completely does it wipe out the personal peculiarities of the actors. In powerful and gripping metaphors, Trotsky sums up:

"To a tickle, people react differently, but to a red-hot iron, alike. As a steam-hammer converts a sphere and a cube alike into sheet-metal, so under the blow of too great and inexorable events resistances are smashed and the boundaries of 'individuality' lost." [1]

[1] *Ibid.*, p. 93.

What Trotsky makes us see is that there are certain historical situations in which the forces unloosed will sweep away anybody who seeks to stop them. Whether these forces are exclusively social and economic, or whether they are compounded with national ambitions and frustrations, religious beliefs and political ambitions, is not important as long as it is recognized that the force of individual personality is no vital part of them.

Reflection will make manifest, however, that, genuine as Trotsky's insight is, it is limited to periods when outbursts of fear or hope sweep over large masses of people, carrying them into action against what until yesterday were the accepted symbols of authority. Where the vital needs of submerged classes are unfulfilled, where conflicts of interest are so deep that they cannot be negotiated without cutting into the vested powers of men who are firmly convinced of their divine or social right to those powers, where customary political rule becomes increasingly inept or oppressive, where the moral professions of those in the saddle sound hollow in the light of actualities—we can already feel the vibrations of discontent that may suddenly erupt into a cataclysmic flood. We can tell that it is coming, we can predict its approach though not what particular event will set it off. We can predict, in other words, the advent of a revolution or war but *not always what its upshot will be. That upshot may sometimes depend upon the characters of the leading personalities.*

This Trotsky does not see, and where he catches a glimpse of the possibility he falters, not knowing whether to abandon his monistic determinism or to force the facts. What his method can explain is at best the death of a system, not what will replace it; the collapse of one culture, not the birth of another; the fall of Czarism, but not the fall of Kerensky or the rise of Bolshevism. It is as if Trotsky, after proving that under certain conditions of cumulative strain and wear an old man must die, were to point to the same conditions as proof that a new life must be born. All men are mortal. But this does not mean that there will always be men. The inescapability of the downfall of Czarism, as we shall see subsequently, does not prove by a long shot the inevitability of the triumph of Bolshevism.

The existence of possible alternatives of development in a historic situation is the presupposition of significant heroic action. The all-important point for our purposes is whether there are such alternatives of development— their nature and duration. The position taken so far commits us to the belief that there have been and are such alternatives in history with mutually incompatible consequences that might have redetermined the course of events in the past, and that might redetermine them in the future. Such a view does not controvert the assumptions of scientific determinism, although it controverts the monistic organic determinism we have previously considered. *For it does not assert that all alternatives are possible.* It recognizes limitations on possibilities, including limitations on the possible effect of heroic action, grounded on the acceptance of generalized descriptions or laws of social behavior.

On the basis of given social data we can sometimes predict the alternatives that are open and those which are closed, although we cannot predict what choice will be made between the open alternatives. For example, the situation of pre-Hitler German economy, with the rolls of its unemployed numbered in millions and steadily mounting from 1928 to 1932, restricted the alternatives to a practical extension of democratic planning for the welfare of the community—a planning which already existed on paper during the Weimar Republic—or to transformation of the national productive plant into an instrument of total war. Whichever alternative was adopted, *and they were both historically possible,* was bound to have a profound effect upon the future development not only of German but of European economy, and its manifold social consequences. The abstract *theoretical* possibility of a return to the free market of early capitalism in Germany was *historically* impossible. The German masses would have starved to death before the free market could have been established.

At the same time it certainly was not a foregone conclusion from what was known of German economy that Hitler's solution would triumph. If greater export possibilities had been opened to the German economy, and if it had not been struck so severely by the crisis, Hitler probably would have failed. But he was victorious not merely because of the widespread economic misery produced by the crisis. His political skill in unifying the right, ranging from Junker to industrialist to the frightened middle classes, together with Hindenburg's support, played an important part. If there had been a great figure in Germany capable of unifying the left and appeasing the center, Hitler might never have become Chancellor.

Where a genuine alternative exists, the active presence of a great man may be decisive—*may be* because *other* elements come into play to decide the issue between the alternatives, and they may weigh more heavily than the element of personality.

Wherever we are in a position to assert, as we shall assert below,[1] that an event-making man has had a decisive influence on a historical period, we are not abandoning the belief in causal connection or embracing a belief in absolute contingency. What we are asserting is that in such situations the great man is a relatively independent historical influence—*independent of the conditions that determine the alternatives*—and that on these occasions the influence of all other relevant factors is of subordinate weight in enabling us to understand or predict which one of the possible alternatives will be actualized. In such situations we also should be able to say, and to present the grounds for saying, that if the great man had *not* existed, the course of events in essential respects would in all likelihood have taken a *different* turn. Those who deny this estimate of the role of the great man in the situation would have to present grounds for the statement that the course of events in essential respects would in all likelihood have taken the same turn. In either case, the fact that we offer grounds for believing what the historical record would be like, *if* some per-

[1] *See* Chapter Ten.

son had not existed, or *if* some event had not transpired, indicates that in the realm of history, as in the realm of nature, pure contingency does not hold sway. *Contingent events in history are of tremendous importance, but the evidence of their importance is possible only because not all events are contingent.*

The whole answer to our inquiry depends upon the legitimacy of our asking and answering—as indeed every competent historian does ask and answer—what would have happened *if* this event had not happened or that man had not lived or this alternative had not been taken. Strangely enough, however, there seems to be a deep-seated reluctance to taking "if" questions in history seriously.[1] They are often dismissed as "purely hypothetical," as if it were self-evident that only nonhypothetical questions were meaningful. The attitude behind these words seems to say: what will be, will be, and what has been, has been, and we need know no more. Yet common discourse is shot through with expressions designed to inquire or to indicate what would have happened *if* an event that actually took place had not occurred. We always have an answer to the person who asks us: "What

[1] Usually rigorous determinists rule "if" questions out as meaningless while extreme indeterminists admit they are meaningful but futile. For example, the French legal philosopher, Tourtoulon, in his discussion of "Possibilities in History," writes: "It is absolutely futile to ask oneself what the world would have become if some particular hypothetical event had been realized, or if some particular real event had not been realized." The reason he offers is that anything might have happened because of the universal sway of chance. Cf. *Philosophy in the Development of Law*, Eng. trans. N. Y. 1922, p. 631. For a contrasting view, cf. M. R. Cohen "Causation and Its Application to History," *Journal of the History of Ideas*, Vol. 3, p. 12ff.

would you now be doing if I had not interrupted you?" History in this respect is no different from ordinary experience even when it has more exalted themes.

It is reported that President Roosevelt at his press conferences sometimes evades embarrassing questions by waving them aside as "iffy." But an "iffy" question, like any other question, may be intelligent or unintelligent, relevant or irrelevant. And as a fool or wise man asks, so should he be answered. But not by denying the validity of this form of question. Were one to ask what the foreign policy of the United States would have been like *if* Wilkie had been elected President in 1940 instead of Roosevelt, we should not have had to be wise only after the event to answer that it would have been the same.

The nature and importance of the problem, and the variety of standpoints adopted toward it, justify our looking more closely at the significance of *if* in history.

VII "If" in History

A FEW YEARS AGO an interesting book was published under the editorship of J. C. Squire. It consisted of a series of studies by distinguished historians and men of letters on some crucial events of history as they might have been.[1] The conception behind the book was brilliant; properly executed, it could have displayed many insights into the dynamics of the historical process. Unfortunately the performance was extremely disappointing. Most of the essays were flights of imagination rather than attempts at scientific reconstruction. Among others, Guedalla speculates on what would have happened if the Moors had won in Spain; H. A. L. Fisher on "If Napoleon Had Escaped to America"; G. K. Chesterton on the marriage of Don John of Austria to Mary Queen of Scots; Nicholson on Byron as King of Greece; Belloc on the successful escape of Louis XVI from revolutionary Paris; Van Loon on continued Dutch rule of New Amsterdam; Winston Churchill on the consequences of a victory by Lee at Gettysburg.

[1] *If or History Rewritten*, New York, 1931.

Under what circumstances can a scientifically credible rather than an imaginatively creditable answer be given to questions of this sort? In order to work out the answer, we shall consider a series of hypothetical situations concerning which we believe credible results can be won. We shall then examine the procedure of these essayists who admit the legitimacy of "if" questions but apparently only as an exercise in imagination, controlled not by historic fact but by the same kind of inherent plausibility exhibited in a well-told story. But prior to this, we must deal with the position that denies it is scientifically meaningful to ask "if" questions.

Some philosophers of history, but no practicing historians, have held that the pattern of historical events is an intricate crisscross of what is technically called "internally related" happenings. Two happenings are internally related if the occurrence of the first necessitates the occurrence of the other, and vice versa. Consequently any change in one will of necessity be followed by a change in the other. The relation of necessity holds between any two events if it is literally impossible for one event to occur if the other does not, or for the first not to occur if the other does. In short, the two events logically entail each other. Now if all events are related to one another in this way, once we assume that *any* event happened differently from what it did—or even that one single detail of it happened differently—every other event would have had to happen differently. But on such a supposition, whenever we ask an "if" question, we cannot intelligently say what would have happened, for *anything* might have happened. We can no longer rely upon relationships observed to hold in other situations to enable us to tell what will now ensue—for these relationships themselves have been automatically altered the very moment we have assumed a hypothesis contrary to fact. From this point of view, all situations or events are mutually interdependent—parts of one total situation or one great event. A hypothesis contrary to fact cannot be stated without self-contradiction. And since it is a self-contradictory statement, anything can be tied to it no matter how fanciful.

This philosophy of history is a specific application of a metaphysical world view. It is occasionally suggested by some forms of theological determinism, but more expressly developed in the Hegelian system of absolute idealism and its variants. It is never carried out consistenly, nor can it ever establish its basic assumptions that all things are necessarily involved in each other and that any true judgment, therefore, entails the totality of all other true judgments. Why, indeed, should the conjoining of any two historical statements like "Wellington fought at Waterloo" (which is in fact true), and "Gold was not discovered in California" (which is in fact false), result in a contradiction? Or can one seriously believe that if my dog whose name is "Trailer" had been called "Tiger" everything else in the world would necessarily have been affected? Here is not the place to criticize in detail the metaphysical theory of the block universe. Its consequences for history reveal its weaknesses sufficiently for present purposes. For it implies that there are no objective possibilities in history, that the future is already actual but unborn, that human effort or the lack of it is predetermined, and that intelligence can never make a difference to what is in the process of becoming but "like the owl of Minerva begins its flight only when the shades of twilight have already fallen" (Hegel).

The degree of interrelatedness between historical events is an empirical matter. When we assert a specific interrelatedness between events, we mean that they are confirming instances of empirical laws that function as hypotheses in the specific problem under inquiry. One way of testing the extent of the interrelation or the validity of the laws is to ask a relevant "if" question. When an answer to the "if" question tells us that the course of events would have followed substantially the same pattern even if the particular occurrence we ask about had not taken place, we may conclude that there is no integral connection between this occurrence and the constellation in which it figures. For example, if Alfred E. Smith had been President in 1928 instead of Hoover, what would the state of American economy have been like during the presidential term? Without any fear of contradiction we can safely answer that it would have been very much like what it was under Hoover. The phases of the business cycle do not depend upon presidential policy. We might even go so far as to say that, no matter who had occupied the White House, in all likelihood the crisis of 1929 and its consequences would have occurred approximately when they did.

On the other hand, suppose we ask whether the social

welfare legislation and the business restrictions associated with the New Deal from 1933 to 1938—measures that banished the era of relatively uncontrolled big business—would have been adopted *if*, by some chance, John Nance Garner had been President during these years. There is no reason to believe that they would have been adopted in anything like their entirety. We can justifiably assert, however, that the failure to adopt remedial economic measures would have resulted in a tremendous growth of indigenous Fascist sentiments and movements out of which a Huey Long could have made great political capital. Sometimes what counts most is the situation, sometimes the man. In 1929 Roosevelt would have been as helpless as Hoover; in 1933 he had his opportunity. He threw his campaign platform of 1932 away because the situation gave him freedom of action, just as Willkie if elected would have thrown away his campaign platform of 1940 because the situation did not give him freedom of action.

*   *   *   *

Citizen Drouet was a modest French provincial who, by dragging a cart across an arched gateway near the bridge at Varennes, foiled the attempt of Louis XVI to flee Paris. The king was in sight of safety when his coach was halted. Hilaire Belloc asks what would have happened if Drouet's cart had stuck and the king had escaped. He blithely answers that the whole history of Europe would have been different, culminating at last in our own day in a "Golden Age of Christendom."

Even for Belloc, whose historical excursions have been one long vendetta against post-Reformation Europe, such a judgment lacks sobriety. He is led to it by the ungrounded assumption that, had he escaped, Louis XVI could have defeated the armies of the Revolution, outgeneraled Napoleon, stopped the consequences of the industrial revolution, and changed not only the leopard spots of capitalism but its very mode of functioning. "Drouet's cart it was that did the trick!" he laments. "Through it the monarchy fell, the Revolution survived, the modern world, its mechanical development and social insecurity became possible." Yet the whole weight of evidence compiled by generations of historians testifies that neither Drouet nor Louis XVI had anything to do with the industrial expansion of Europe in the late eighteenth century and its vast ramification of social effects. Belloc places too great a weight of historical interrelatedness on two inconsequential pivots, royal and common.

*   *   *   *

A much more topical "if" question is provided by the situation of Napoleon poised on the English Channel ready to strike at England. What would have happened if, on a day that the English fleet was becalmed, Napoleon had steamed across the Channel and realized his long-unfulfilled dream of invading England? Would Napoleon have avoided his Waterloo, and would England have been transformed into a French province?

The following excerpts from two communications prove that the possibility of Napoleon's steaming across the Channel was not far-fetched, but hung on a thread of bureaucratic red tape. The first is from a letter of Robert Fulton, the inventor of the steamboat, to Napoleon: "I can remove the obstacles—wind and storm—which protect your enemies, and, notwithstanding his fleet, transport your armies to his territory at any time, and within a few hours." The second is from a letter of Napoleon to his Minister of the Interior on July 21, 1804. The date is significant because it indicates the years Napoleon had before him in which to avail himself of Fulton's invention: "I have just read the proposition of the Citizen Fulton, engineer, which you have sent me much too late, since it is one which may change the whole face of the world. Submit it instantly for examination to a special committee." [1]

Let us assume that Fulton's invention had not been buried in committee but had been acted upon, a fleet of steam transports equipped, and Napoleon's army ferried across the Channel. Would his invasion have been successful? Whatever our answer, it will have to be made in terms of certain principles or laws of military warfare as these have been established in comparable situations. Since an army lives on its stomach, supplies, and reinforcements, Napoleon would have had to keep open at all costs his line of communications. So long as the British fleet remained in existence, that would have been impossible. Since he could not count on the wind to hold the English fleet permanently becalmed, he would have had

---

[1] Both excerpts are quoted in Carola Oman's *Napoleon at the Channel*, p. 155, New York, 1942.

to destroy it. By the time he had equipped a steam battle
fleet, the English with their greater shipbuilding and industrial capacities would have met him on at least equal
terms. We may, therefore, conclude that even if Napoleon had landed in England, he would still have been far
from victory. This conclusion would, of course, be much
more assured if he had managed to reach the English
shore only with sailing vessels.

*   *   *   *

One of the most famous of all "if" questions was originally raised by the German historian, Eduard Meyer,
and used as a key illustration by Max Weber in his discussion of "objective possibility" in history. What would
the subsequent history of Europe have been like *if* the
Persian hosts had been victorious at the battles of Marathon, Salamis, and Platea? Meyer maintains with justification that the political history as well as the cultural
values of Greek and European civilization would have
been profoundly different from the legacy that has come
down to us. Since the settled policy of the Achaemenian
Empire was to impose its own autocratic and priestly
rule upon the territories subjugated by its armies, the
Greek city-state with its traditions of autonomy and
limited democracy would in all likelihood have disappeared from Europe, and the great efflorescence of Greek
culture that followed the emancipation from fear of the
Persian yoke would have been frozen in the bud. Most
but not all historians of the ancient world agree with this.
James Breasted follows Meyer there, but H. A. L. Fisher,

the English historian, believes that the Persian victory would not have undermined genuine Greek traditions because both Darius and Xerxes were prepared to use renegade Greeks as puppet rulers. Under these puppet Greek rulers, what was distinctive in Greek culture would have been preserved.

But this overlooks the fact that not all Greeks were devoted to the Greek city-state any more than all Frenchmen accept the heritage of the French Revolution. Some Greeks preferred the stability of Persian despotism to the turbulence of Greek democracy. In addition, Fisher disregards the ruthless punitive measures taken by the Persians against the revolting Ionian cities and all who aided them. The same fate would have befallen the rest of the Greek cities if the Persian tide had broken through their defense.

The possibility envisaged by Meyer is credible and likely because it is based on the settled political and military policy of the Achaemenian Empire, as evidenced in a whole series of other actions in its history. That this policy would have remained constant is, of course, an assumption. But there is no reason to justify the belief that it would have been abandoned by a triumphant Xerxes, while there are good reasons for believing that such a policy, where it could be enforced, strengthened the Persians. If we are not justified in making assumptions concerning the relative constancy of certain determinate relationships in any historical situation, it would be hard to draw a line between fantasy and scientific reconstruction.

A disregard of this line between fantasy and scientific reconstruction mars at every crucial point Winston Churchill's well-told tale of the result of hypothetical Confederate victory at Gettysburg. The high points in his hypothetical account of the consequences of a lost battle at Gettysburg are: (1) defeat of the North and the peaceful existence of two nations in the area now comprising the United States; (2) Lee's abolition of slavery, immediately after the victory at Gettysburg, which reconciled the North to peace and brought an alliance between England and the South; (3) the formation at a moment of crisis around 1905 of an English Speaking Association, "The Re-United States" of Britain, the North, and the South—one great union of the Anglo-Saxon peoples, "members of one body and inheritors of one estate"; (4) the peaceful resolution of the incident at Sarajevo in 1914 by the open threat of the English Speaking Union to declare war against any power whose troops invaded a neighboring country.

1. The military consequences to the North of a lost battle at Gettysburg would have included not a lost war but a prolonged one. The industrial equipment of the North, its much denser population, its command of the sea—not to mention the fall of Vicksburg and the control this gave of the Mississippi—spelled defeat in the end for the South. The capture of Washington and the threat to the Northern States would have unified sentiment in those regions and led to a more vigorous prosecution of the war. It might even have converted Lincoln into a Radical Republican. We agree with Churchill that "Once

a great victory is won . . . all the chains of consequence clink out as if they never would stop." But a victorious war for the South would not have been a link in the chain of consequences of a Northern military defeat. If great victories had been able to ensure final triumph in the Civil War, the South would have won easily, since it won most of the battles, as did the German Imperial forces in the First World War. If disastrous military defeats of the magnitude hypothetically suffered by the North were always a prelude to a lost war, there would today be no British Empire.

2. That Lee would have proclaimed the emancipation of the slaves after a Confederate victory at Gettysburg is a pretty conceit of a dramatic historian. There were plenty of victorious battles in whose wake he could have done this but did not. He did not because it would have disrupted the plantation economy in whose behalf the Southern States went to war. That England would have actively intervened on the side of the South in the event of a victory at Gettysburg is unlikely. So far as the working-class population was concerned, its sympathies were actively for the North. To the extent that foreign policy in the hands of the ruling classes could proceed independently of this sentiment, the line of diplomatic strategy during the century was to play off one side against the other in order to weaken both—not only in the Civil War but in every war on the Continent.

3. To believe that in 1905 two mutually jealous sovereign states, the United States of the North and the Confederate States of the South, whose interests conflicted at

many points, would surrender their sovereignty for union with a third, the United Kingdom of Great Britain,—regarded as a hereditary enemy by at least one of them—is a tribute to Mr. Churchill's high hopes and aspirations, not to his insight as a historian. It has no precedent in human history. Its failure to take place would be more in keeping with the record. Indeed, it would certainly have been much easier to achieve union between the indivisible United States and Great Britain after the First World War in which they were close allies. Nothing like it ever happened, or was officially proposed, or was even suggested until the time of Mr. Churchill's essay. On the basis of this essay, however, he must be credited with being the original, albeit indirect, sponsor of the program of Union Now.

That an event has no precedent in human history is not, of course, an objection to its occurrence. Otherwise there would be no history. But the likelihood of such an event depends upon the nature of the situation that leads up to it. The Union that Mr. Churchill envisages in his reconstructed tale was unlikely because at the time there was nothing to lead up to it in terms of common history, activity, and interests. It comes as a suggestion out of the blue. Because at the *present* time the situation is different in these respects, his idea is an objective historical possibility even if it is *not* acted upon.

4. It is undoubtedly true that the First World War would not have broken out in August 1914 if a union of English-speaking nations had delivered its ultimatum to Europe. There is evidence that Germany definitely

counted on English-American neutrality during the time assigned by its High Command for finishing off France and Russia. Nonetheless it would have required more than an English-American *démarche* to banish the likelihood of a better-prepared-for war in the next few years, even if the crisis of 1914 had been peacefully settled. What was required was a permanent solution of the Balkan problem, agreement of all interested parties on the existence and control of the Berlin-Bagdad railroad, a redivision of the raw materials and colonial markets of the world, Germany's return to Bismarck's naval policy, and considerable military disarmament all around—not to speak of profound modifications in the internal capitalist economy of the major powers. There is not the slightest evidence that these requirements stood an appreciable chance of being fulfilled.

* * * *

One of the recurrent weaknesses of the imaginative reconstructions of a hypothetical past is that the line of inference is often drawn too far into the future. Not satisfied with reconstructing the given situation for a limited period, in which the succession of alternative happenings can be clearly envisaged, those who think through the process of reconstruction carry it indefinitely forward. They therewith tend to disregard the increasing possibilities of alternate developments as more and more elements enter the story. If a reconstruction over a period of a few years is risky, a reconstruction over a period of a hundred years is much more than ten times as risky. The following illustrations may make this clearer.

If Quebec had fallen to American assault in the War of Independence, we can safely predict that the war would have ended sooner than it did and that Benedict Arnold would have escaped the fate of a traitor. It is a safe prediction but not necessarily true because we are assuming that certain generalizations about the conduct of war and the behavior of individuals like Arnold are valid. Although we have a right to make these generalizations on the basis of rules derived from past experience, we have no logical guarantee that they will continue to hold or that something new and completely unforeseen will not crop up to prolong the war and make a traitor of Arnold. We are assuming that other occurrences, happenings in other series of events unrelated to the series that followed the fall of Quebec, will not intersect the latter. But they may. That is why our judgment is well grounded and reliable but not certain. We can also predict, but not so safely, that if Quebec had fallen the Canadian provinces, with their large French population only recently transferred to the English flag, would have raised no insuperable objection at the end of the war to incorporation in the United States of America. Here the possible number of disturbing elements from other series of events is larger, and the period of time over which they could interfere with what would otherwise have been the case is greater. But if anyone were to try to predict the effect of the incorporation of Canada upon the development of American economy and politics down to the twentieth century, his conclusions would be extremely improbable although not necessarily fanciful. He could make out a one-way case for the development of the series of events in relative isolation from other series of events, but we can see, on the basis of our knowledge of other histories, a vast number of other series of events that could have intersected at many points the hypothetical history.

If there had been no Reformation, we could safely predict that there would have been no Counter Reformation, that is, that many of the events which occurred in the seventeenth century would not have taken place. True enough. But if there had been no Reformation, would we now be enjoying tolerance under a universal religion of free-thinking Popes who interpreted sacred Biblical history as morally edifying fairy tales—as Santayana apparently believes? Many other things would have had *not* to happen before this kind of civilized culture could have developed. So many, indeed, that we can dismiss the suggestion as fanciful.

It is safe to predict, that is, offer valid grounds for asserting, that if at Versailles in 1919 either the policy of Clemenceau or that of Wilson had been followed to the bitter end, instead of compounding the weaknesses of both, the rest of the world would have had less to fear from Hitler. But if Saul had remained Saul or if, reborn as Paul, he had not decided to bring the gospel of the Messiah, crucified and risen, to the Gentiles, what would have been the fate of the Roman Empire, of Europe under Alaric and other barbarian chiefs, of France in the

eighteenth century, assuming that there were a France?
Would modern science and democracy have developed
earlier or not at all? Here only the sketchiest answers can
be made with good sense.[1]

When we draw the line of possible eventuality too far
out of the immediate period, the mind staggers under the
cumulative weight of the unforeseen. That is why prophecy is such a hazardous vocation. We are more alive to
the chances of the future because they are still before us,
but the past, too, even though it is over, is an exciting
story of chances missed. The past closes silently behind
us with the awful finality of a divine judgment. But the
finality means that historical events are irreversible, not
that they are all necessary and certainly not that they are
all good. A deceptive backward glance mistakes the unforeseen for the predetermined. The hypnotic influence of
the long-established, of what cannot be changed, often
misleads the innocent into believing that it has a hidden
purpose and the pious into the blasphemy that the judgment of history is the judgment of God.

If we seek understanding and not salvation from the
pages of history, we will not fail to recognize the might-
have-beens of the past. Some of them may turn out as
relevant to the chances of the future as a recognized mis-
take is to the successful action that follows it. These

---

[1] This is the drawback of all reconstructions of prolonged historical
periods, such as Charles Renouvier's *Uchronie—L'Utopie dans l'His-
toire*, in which he gives us an account of European civilization from
the second century to the seventeenth "not as it was, but as it might
have been." Such reconstructions, although of dubious scientific value,
may have great moral and pedagogical significance.

might-have-beens of history are not ghostly echoes of what people merely hoped for, but objective possibilities that were missed—sometimes for want of a hero, sometimes for want of a horse, sometimes for want of a shoe, but most of the time for want of intelligence, particularly in realizing the objective possibilities of good.

We may compare the process of history to a gnarled ancient tree, still in healthy growth, whose trunk is the human race with interlacing boughs arching in many directions. Along each bough, large and then smaller limbs branch off, down to the very twigs. Here and there signs point to a branch of a twin stem that had been lopped off, while its other has grown to tremendous dimensions. At other places, what started out as an independent bough rounds off to a knotty protuberance. Under its mass of foliage, dead, rotting limbs can be found. A skillful gardener might once have trimmed it into a symmetrical form or other pleasing shapes, but the job would be difficult now. And it would have to be repeated yearly, for new shoots are put forth every season. It is exposed to quick destruction by lightning and to slow death by poisonous fungi. And there is no common agreement about the taste of its fruit.

We can easily imagine boughs of the tree in places where there are none now, less easily the branches that might have forked from these absent boughs, but we can guess only wildly at where the twigs and leaves would stem off from our imagined branches. We can easily see when we look at the living tree, more readily than when we experience living history, because our eyes trace a geometrical pattern, that if any of the actual boughs had not developed or had been destroyed, everything that grew on it and out of it would be nonexistent. From this it does not follow, as we have seen, that the trunk "explains" the bough, the bough the branch, the branch the twig, the twig the leaf. The first is only the necessary condition of the second.

The architectural pattern of the tree is much simpler than the causal relationships of history. The tree of history has no "true" or "necessary" or "predetermined" or "fixed" shape. Neither has it an infinite variety of branchings without law or pattern or mutual support and interrelation. It is not a patch of tangled wilderness where nothing leads anywhere and anything can grow at any place.

VIII *The Contingent and the Unforeseen*

THE RELATIVE SIZE of things depends upon perspective. The scrub oak and the towering maple that contrast so sharply in the valley are hardly distinguishable when viewed from the mountaintop. Similarly, when we survey the fortunes of a people from a great distance, important facts of variety are overlooked, and the disparities between great men and little are flattened out.

To the question: what is the proper perspective from which history should be viewed—a year, a decade, a century, or a millennium?, our answer must be that there is no such thing as a "proper" perspective independent of a problem. The posing of the problem already presupposes that we have limited our inquiry to a definite time span. For purposes of comparative analysis, an intelligible account of an entire culture can be written in brief compass, without reference to the causal influences of outstanding personalities or to other contingent happenings. But it does not follow from this that the history of any limited period within the culture can dispense with such references.

To a mind sensitive to possibilities and lovingly curious of detail, the aspect of contingency in history will loom much larger than to those whose eyes make century sweeps over the record. When we view the life of a man, not as it appears to a biographer, but as a history of a human being compared to a history of the earth, the seas, or the stars, it can be described in simple formulas. These will not say much more than did the Chinese counselors to their aging emperor, who early in his reign had set them to fathom "the secret" of man. On his deathbed they reported to him that man is born, lives, suffers, and dies. Change any detail of his life, make him beggar or king, warrior or saint, and it still remains true. Change the man, his country, his period, the same pattern can be traced in all the changes. Such reflections are relevant to the human estate in which each man counts for any other; applied to the history of any particular man they are worthless except where the tale would make us believe that he is more than man.

If we chart the history of human societies with calipers that stretch over millenia can we, from that perspective, say much more than that they, too, have a common pattern and fate? They are born, grow more or less powerful, weaken, and disappear. With a strong government, they last a little longer; with a wise government, the condition of their members is a little more livable; with a religious government, more of their members die in the odor of sanctity or as heretics at the stake. But they all run the same course—Greece and Persia, Rome and Jerusalem, the societies of Saladin and of Richard I. If this were all the wisdom that could be found in the cyclical theories of Vico, Hegel, Spengler, and Toynbee, they would not be worth reading. The Book of Ecclesiastes would be enough.

Historical enlightenment is not furthered by approaching cultures as *wholes* and trying to explain them in their entirety. Nor can everything about cultures be understood by intuiting them as "unique totalities of meaning." Historical understanding is furthered by isolating specific problems of connection within cultures or of interaction between cultures; by tracing structural interrelations and temporal dependencies between the institutions found within a culture; and by showing how determinate phases and changes of a culture are conditioned by features of the noncultural environment of man. It is doubtful whether anyone knows what he means, or has accurately expressed what he means, when he requests an explanation of Greek culture as a whole or of the entire course of American history. To be historically significant, the uniformities alleged to hold for cultures must go beyond the inadequate metaphors of the cycle of birth, maturity, and decay. They must point to specific mechanisms, to controlling conditions, to causal influences weighted in a certain order—in short, to those recurrent aspects of ever-fresh experience on the basis of which we can predict and act intelligently.

But, then, what happens to the contingent, the unique, the individual, and the novel about which we have previously spoken? Do they not all slip through the meshes of our understanding? Does not the "historicity" of the historical vanish whenever we explain a specific historical event in terms of general relations, functions, causes? This question has given rise to a great deal of discussion, but part of the difficulty lies in the ambiguity of the term "contingent." The contingent in one sense is that which is given or found, whose existence is not logically necessary and whose nonexistence is not logically impossible. In this sense everything that exists is contingent, as are the laws that describe the way contingent things are related. In another sense, the contingent is the irrelevant. Once we discover a law relating classes of things, from the point of view of this law, the phenomena that are unrelated to it are contingent. And no law can be found that describes the behavior of some things without the assumption of the irrelevance of other things. In a third sense (a special case of the second) an event is contingent if it occurs as a consequence of the intersection of two series of events, described by laws that are irrelevant to each other.[1]

In the primary sense of the term, we can admit the existence of the contingent in every individual event, but it does not therefore follow that everything about the event is contingent or novel. In the secondary sense we can legitimately predict that an event will occur as a consequence of a series of earlier ones and yet find that

[1] Cf. Morris R. Cohen, *Reason and Nature*, pp. 151-152, New York, 1932. Also Cournot, *Considérations sur La Marche des Idées et des Evenéments dans Les Temps Modernes*, ed. by Mentré, vol. I., pp. 1-15.

because of the interposition of another series of events
what we expected turned out otherwise—a good or bad
"accident."

Historians who are immersed in the rich details of historical events, and who are often brought up short by the
unexpectedness of happenings, sometimes exaggerate the
element of contingency to a point where history appears
to them as *nothing but* a story of the unexpected. The
"great man" as well as everything else appears contingent
so that in their account he plays no greater role than in
the account of the extreme determinist. In consequence,
the problem of what specific historical effect a particular individual has at any definite time is a problem that,
on this view, can hardly be stated. One contingency is
born of another, and who can say where it leads and
why. Such historians do not distinguish between three
different things: the tautology that the absolutely novel
aspect of an event cannot be understood or predicted;
the view that the interrelationships between events show
such complexity that intelligible explanations and predictions cannot be made; and the view that the contingent can only have historical effects because of what
is not contingent.

In a famous passage of an impressive historical work, a
distinguished English scholar claims that the only uniformity the practicing historian can legitimately recognize in human development is "the play of the contingent
and unforeseen."

One intellectual excitement, however, has been denied
me. Men wiser and more learned than I have discerned

in History a plot, a rhythm, a pre-determined pattern. These harmonies are concealed from me. I can see only one emergency following upon another as wave follows wave; only one great fact, with respect to which, since it is unique, there can be no generalizations; only one safe rule for the historian: that he should recognize in the development of human destinies the play of the contingent and unforeseen. This is not a doctrine of cynicism or despair. . . .[1]

The view expressed in the passage is so widely held that it will repay closer study. As it stands there is a certain ambiguity in it. If it is taken to express Mr. Fisher's disbelief in·some kind of theological determinism like that of Augustine and Tolstoy, or of the purposive idealism of Hegel and the dialectical materialists, no one interested in scientific history can take objection to it. Yet events that follow each other "as wave follows wave" certainly suggest a rhythm which in any case is different from the meaning of a plot and the finality of a predetermined pattern. And although a thing may be unique— our earth, for example—there are many generalizations that may validly be applied to it. But the author's basic meaning is clear—and mistaken. The "one" great fact of contingency that he stresses is no more basic or important than another great fact, *viz.*, the *limits* of contingency in human affairs.

Chains of consequences are not strictly necessary, but we may count upon them nine times out of ten, and often more frequently. Introduce technology into a cul-

[1] H. A. L. Fisher, *A History of Europe*, vol. I, p. vii, London, 1935.

ture, even one hostile to the foreign values associated with technology, and a whole series of effects, from the establishment of an armament industry to political centralization, will ensue. Humiliate a defeated enemy without utterly destroying his potential powers of rearmament, and there will be another war in a generation. Let a nation wax fat and grow pacific while its neighbor remains hungry but well armed, and the prosperous country will be overrun as soon as a plausible pretext can be found. If those who start a civil war fight only defensive battles, it is only a matter of time before their cause is lost. Call a general strike without setting a limit to its duration, and the strike will fail. Let a democratic organization make a united front with a disciplined totalitarian organization that agitates for its own program, and the democratic body will either become a catspaw for purposes foreign to its democratic aims or meet organizational disaster.

Of course every situation will to some extent be different. That is what we *mean* when we say we can distinguish between two situations. We can go beyond this tautology. We can admit that the contingent and unforeseen, eruptions from outside into the pattern of expectation, almost invariably crop up. But it will not do to count upon them to stave off a disaster that can be spelled out from what we have previously done. We can be sure that something will always turn up, but not always in the right place. What is truly unique about the contingent and unforseen is that it always can be anticipated but never relied upon.

That the variations in contingent historical effects are limited by certain "laws" of historical behavior is recognized at every hand in the body of the work which the cited passage introduces. In fact, I am acquainted with few historical accounts that are studded with so many laws and generalizations—some of quite questionable validity—about the limits within which the contingent and unforeseen are to be found. We introduce them as illustrations, not because we accept them as true, but to show that Mr. Fisher must believe them to be true, or something like them to be true, in order to compose an intelligible story.

In speaking of the periodic raids of the early Greek settlers, he tells us: "The quest of supplies by war or plunder was a *necessary* supplement to the tillage and pasturage of the community. It was not so much a crime as a part of state economy. Man must eat to live. If crops run short, he *must* steal, fight or emigrate." Of the course of Roman expansion, he writes: "The successive stages of her conquest of Italy were *forced* upon her because, as England afterwards experienced in India, an orderly power ringed round by turbulence *always* finds itself compelled to establish peace and security upon its frontiers." And of the effect of this expansion, in its later phases, on Roman character he adds: "The vast plunder of Africa and Asia, of Macedonia and Greece, produced upon the Roman character the evil effects which suddenly acquired wealth *always* exerts upon minds unprepared to receive it."

Mr. Fisher is not a historical materialist or an economic

determinist, but he has such a healthy respect for the "laws" of political economy that he gives them sway over the entire realm of historical contingency. Thus ". . . Diocletian, one of the wisest of the Emperors, issued an edict fixing prices all over the Empire, and found, as many have found since his day, that *not all the laws or penalties in the world can prevent* men from buying in the cheapest and selling in the dearest market." What is true for the time of Diocletian is also true eleven hundred years later for England after the Black Death: "In England Parliament called laborers and artisans to their old rate of wages and forbade them to move from one country to another. Political economy, like nature, may be expelled with a fork, but it *always* returns. The legislation of the Edwardian parliaments was unavailing to arrest a process grounded in the economic *necessities* of the time." [1]

Expressions like "necessary," "forced upon," "always," "must," and "cannot" are no part of the language of contingency, not to mention those rhetorical flights in which Sulla's reform of the Roman Senate is pronounced doomed, since "what neither Sulla nor anyone else could do was to fight against the stars in their courses."

Every contingent fact makes a break in a web of historical relationships that determines how far it shall fall. All that we need to vindicate here is the fact that the web is often broken, and that a great man may be one of the contingent phenomena that break it.

[1] These quotations are from the work cited, vol. I, pp. 18, 62, 64, 93, 320. All italics mine.

What has been demonstrated for Fisher can be established as easily by examining the pages of any historian who magnifies the facts of contingency at the expense of its limits.

*   *   *   *

We have previously seen that "if" questions in history are scientifically meaningful. It can also be shown that they point to a fact of tremendous moral and social significance. The necessities of history as of nature, with which it is continuous, are binding without being logically compelling. The necessities of history, where they can be distinguished from those of nature, are in part purposive. They contain an implicit reference to what human beings regard as valuable or preferable.

When we say that the abolition of slavery was historically necessary or that the liberation of productive forces from the restrictions of private monopoly is a social necessity, there are at least two things involved. The first is certain assumptions about the biological and psychological nature of man as they appear in a social context. The properties of human behavior are taken to be *relatively* invariant, of the same general character but of a specifically different subject matter as the properties investigated by any natural science.

The second reference is to the order of human values and preferences which obtain at the time, to a choice between evils and goods, to a policy of dealing with the given conditions. The order, the choice, the policy may themselves be the predictable result of habit, education, and tradition. But since they are voluntary, they may also be the consequence of intelligent reflection—and in that sense a free determination. This free determination cuts down but can never eliminate the hazards of the future. If, as Hans Reichenbach suggests, every act of ours is a wager against a possible disappointment, the method of intelligence is a method of increasing the odds in our favor.

Many of the might-have-beens of history were beyond human control. It is hard to see what human beings could have done to realize these might-have-beens prior to the decisive events that finally sentenced them to indeterminate status in limbo. We are gratified that the assassin's bullet missed President Roosevelt in 1933: we deplore the fact that the Reichswehr volley left Hitler alive in the Munich putsch of 1923. The grounded possibility of a hit in both instances brings home to us the complexity of all historical processes at the same time as it reinforces our sense of helplessness in relation to it. Remembered in season, the grounded, objective possibilities that are outside the scope of human control tend to loosen the rigid formulas of the theorist and curb the natural dogmatism of the man of action. Properly considered, they can fortify us against the sting of defeats imposed upon us by chance and hard luck.

But, as we have seen, other might-have-beens were within human grasp. They are the genuinely lost chances, for they *could* have been. They were lost because of the failure to be more intelligent, more courageous, more resolute—sometimes a little more of each.

The triumphs of intelligence and will never violate natural and social necessities. They tap unsuspected potential resources of mind and body the better to cope with these necessities. Intelligence and will supply by their own effort some of the conditions upon which the transition from the "might be" to the "is" hangs. That is what we mean when we say retrospectively that the impossible has been achieved. Among the most poignant tragedies of history are those in which men have cried "impossible" too soon, and for want of vision have summoned up energies sufficient to win the day—too late. The virtues and vices of men are more than catalytic agents. They can be and have been powerful historical forces, a fact which gainsays no intelligent conception of social determinism.

Moral responsibility in history consists in being aware of the relevant *ifs* and *might-be's* in the present, and choosing between alternatives in the light of predictable consequences. We may lose even after we have chosen intelligently and fought bravely. In that case regret is always vain, and resignation, without capitulation to the ideals of the enemy, is the better part of wisdom, until a new opportunity supervenes. But intelligence and sustained courage will win much more often than drift and fitful bursts of effort. If there is any ethical imperative valid for all historical periods it is awareness and action.

These reflections have a particular bearing on our own historical present. Wherever we look at the world today, we can observe the fateful consequences of the lost chances of yesterday. The international labor and socialist movement lost its chance in August 1914 to stop a world war that, as was predicted then, would breed more terrible wars. Kerensky and the democratic socialist bloc lost the chance to put into effect the official but unannounced program of his own party which, as Chernov has revealed, called for cessation of war, the distribution of land to the peasants, and other measures that the Bolsheviks advocated as preparatory to imposing their ruthless minority dictatorship. The leading party of the Weimar Republic lost its chance to break up the monarchist centers of reaction without whose help Hitler might never have come to power. The governments of western Europe and the United States lost their chance to help the legally recognized Spanish state against invasion by Mussolini and Hitler and win an active ally on the Continent instead of a hostile neutral, in the inescapable showdown with Fascism.

The consequences of a lost chance rarely close the doors to future choice. But they narrow them to alternatives that are all relatively unfavorable in comparison with earlier possibilities. The justification of the present war against Fascism is not to be found in resurrected echoes of a Wilsonian idealism which lost its chance at Versailles to redeem its promises. It is to be found in the fact that defeat at the hands of the Axis spells universal Fascism and its unspeakable barbarity and degradation, while victory over it means survival and one more chance. One more chance to solve the basic problem of our time—the fusion of the economic tendency toward a planned economy with the values and techniques of democracy. Fascism or democratic survival and another chance—this is the grim alternative of our time.

IX The Eventful Man and the Event-Making Man

THROUGHOUT THIS BOOK we have been using the word "hero" in the rather large and vague sense given to it in common usage. It is now necessary to make the term sufficiently precise to permit some check upon the position that will be subsequently developed.

Before proceeding to the main distinction upon which our thesis hangs, it will be helpful to introduce a few secondary distinctions that have been alluded to in earlier chapters. First of all, we must distinguish between the hero of historical action and the hero of thought. Popular estimates of "great" or "eminent" men rarely differentiate between the two. Thus in the well-known survey made by J. McKeen Cattell on the outstanding figures in western history, the ten who headed the list of a thousand names were: Napoleon, Shakespeare, Mohammed, Voltaire, Bacon, Aristotle, Goethe, Caesar, Luther, and

Plato.[1] But as far as the records of historical events go, only four out of this group can be considered as candidates for the role of historical hero. No one can plausibly maintain that Shakespeare had any influence on the occurrence or nonoccurrence of decisive historical events. It is not precluded that heroes of thought might also be great men of action or that the consequences of their ideas, as in the case of inventors, religious leaders, and social philosophers, might have impressive historical effects. But it is to the record of events that we must turn to evaluate their claims. In the history of the ancient world, it is Alexander, whose name does not appear on the list, who emerges as a historical hero rather than Aristotle. Only if it could be shown that it was Aristotle's ideas that inspired Alexander in his march toward empire could the former be considered in this connection.

A second distinction must be recognized between historical figures who are famous, who can get themselves believed in, and individuals who have influenced events without achieving great popular fame. There is no reliable correlation between historical significance, measured by the effect of action on events, and historical fame, measured by acclaim or volume of eulogy. That is why the judgment of the scientific historian, who investigates specific causal connection, on the historical work of individuals, is always to be preferred to results of polls, comparative space allotments in standard works,

[1] *Popular Science Monthly*, vol. 62 (1903), p. 359. This study was based on the comparative space allotted to a thousand pre-eminent men in standard biographical dictionaries and encyclopedias.

and frequency of citation. The latter show enormous variation influenced by fashion, picturesqueness, *parti pris*, and very little by scientific findings. Particularly today, any "front" man can be built up into a "hero." From 1916 to 1933, Hindenburg was undoubtedly the most popular figure in Germany but one could mention half a dozen individuals who had greater influence on German history, including military history, during that period.

Finally, we must rule out as irrelevant the conception of the hero as a morally worthy man, not because ethical judgments are illegitimate in history, but because so much of it has been made by the wicked. Only the making of history concerns us here, not whether it has been made well or disastrously.

The hero in history is the individual to whom we can justifiably attribute preponderant influence in determining an issue or event whose consequences would have been profoundly different if he had not acted as he did. It is sometimes objected that there is no universal agreement about the "importance" of any issue, event, or consequences. Some individuals profess that it is not "important" to them whether India remains free or not, whether the war is lost or won, or whether the future world state is democratic or Fascist in form. All this is immaterial to the problem. No matter what *you* regard as important, the problem is inescapable. Would that which *you* regard as important have taken place anyhow no matter what individual figured in the events leading up to it? Or is it ever true to say that an individual was chiefly responsible for the occurrence or nonoccurrence of that important issue or event?

This brings us to the key distinction. This is the distinction between the hero as the *eventful man* [1] in history and the hero as the *event-making man* in history. The *eventful* man in history is any man whose actions influenced subsequent developments along a quite different course than would have been followed if these actions had not been taken. The *event-making* man is an eventful man whose actions are the consequences of outstanding capacities of intelligence, will, and character rather than of accidents of position. This distinction tries to do justice to the general belief that a hero is great not merely in virtue of what he does but in virtue of what he is. From this point on, unless otherwise specified, when we speak of the hero or great man in history we shall mean the event-making man.

The merely eventful men in history play a role that may be compared to that of the little Dutch boy who kept his finger in the hole of the dikes and saved the town. Without meaning to strip the legend of its glamor, we can point out that almost anybody in the situation could have done it. All that was required was a boy, a finger, and the lucky chance of passing by. The event itself in the life of the community was of tremendous significance. It saved the town just as a little Dutch boy at Pearl Harbor might have saved the fleet if his alarm had been acted upon in time. But the qualities required to

[1] I owe the expression "eventful man" to Mr. Charles Haer, who is, however, in no way responsible for the position here developed.

cope with the situation were of a fairly common distribution. Here, so to speak, one stumbles upon greatness just as one might stumble on a treasure that will ransom a town. Greatness, however, is something that must involve extraordinary talent of some kind and not merely the compounded luck of being born and of being present at the right place at a happy moment.

In the year 313, the Emperor Constantine, in the words of Gibbon, changed his status from that of "protector" to that of "proselyte" of the Church.[1] Few events have been more important in the development of western Europe than the reversal of previous Roman policy toward Christianity and its adoption by the official head of the Roman Empire. But not a single one of the qualities of Constantine's character, which enter into the disputed question of the reasons for his conversion, indicate that he was much more than a politician with an eye on the main chance. Whatever religious piety he had was not strong enough to prevent him from murdering his own son on a trumped-up charge. Constantine was an eventful man independently of whether Christianity would have become the official religion several centuries later, under quite different conditions and with different consequences, or whether, without him, the Roman Empire would never have been called Holy. But as decisive as Constantine's act was for his era, *he* was not a hero. The appellation of "great" was bestowed upon him in thanks by the grateful Christian minority. His later inter-

[1] Edward Gibbon, *History of the Decline and Fall of the Roman Empire*, Modern Library edition, vol. I, p. 636.

ference in church affairs gave them second thoughts about his greatness.

Although there is no evidence that any other Roman Emperor would have eased Christianity into its new status, it could have been done readily. The growth of Christianity, the position of the Emperor in Roman society, the decay in traditional belief manifested by the absence of a strong, fanatical opposition, made the adoption of Christianity an objective possibility, but neither a social nor political necessity. Constantine proselytized for Christianity for imperial reasons.[1] But there was no greater justification for believing that he could strengthen the state by using the church primarily as an instrument of public policy than by playing off Paganism and Christianity against each other. *After* Constantine and his work, and *because* of it, the effort to restore the pagan religion was doomed to fail. It is extremely unlikely that the Emperor Julian, despite his superior gifts, would have succeeded in depriving Christianity of its privileged status even if he had lived to a ripe age. But what he failed to do as a successor of Constantine—reduce Christianity to a religious sect contending on equal terms against other sects—he could easily have done in Constantine's stead. Constantine, therefore, must be regarded as an eventful rather than an event-making historical figure.

Both the eventful man and the event-making man appear at the forking points of history. The possibility of

[1] Cf. C. N. Cochrane, *Christianity and Classical Culture*, p. 211, Oxford, 1940.

their action has already been prepared for by the direction of antecedent events. The difference is this. In the case of the eventful man, the preparation is at a very advanced stage. It requires a relatively simple act—a decree, a command, a common-sense decision—to make the decisive choice. He may "muff" his role or let someone steal it from him. But even if he doesn't, this does not prove him an exceptional creature. His virtue or vice is inferred from the happy or unhappy consequence of what he has done, not from the qualities he has displayed in the doing of it.

The event-making man, on the other hand, finds a fork in the historical road, but he also helps, so to speak, to create it. He increases the odds of success for the alternative he chooses by virtue of the extraordinary qualities he brings to bear to realize it. At the very least, like Caesar and Cromwell and Napoleon, he must free the path he has taken from opposition and, in so doing, display exceptional qualities of leadership. It is the hero as event-making man who leaves the positive imprint of his personality upon history—an imprint that is still observable after he has disappeared from the scene. The merely eventful man whose finger plugs a dike or fires the shot that starts a war is rarely aware of the nature of the alternative he faces and of the train of events his act sets off.

It is easy to make a sharp distinction in analysis between the eventful man and the event-making man, but there are few historical figures that will fit snugly into either classification. We must leave to historians the delicate task of ascertaining whether any particular "hero" of human history is, in respect to some significant happening, an event-making character—or merely lucky. That the classes defined by the distinction are not empty of members has been made apparent for eventful men and will be established for event-making men. Whether it is possible to treat these classes in terms of gradations or combinations of qualities common to both is doubtful. Yet the same historical personage may be eventful in one respect, event-making in another, and neither in a third.

It is not suggested that this approach is the only one that can be taken in evaluating the historical significance of individuals in history. For the nature of their influence may be expressed in ways so manifold that they sum up to a torrent, and yet at the same time in ways so indirect that it is difficult to trace their path.

The influence of Thomas Jefferson and Abraham Lincoln on American life, on the ways Americans have thought and acted, has been enormous. Yet it would be difficult, and perhaps irrelevant, to classify them either as eventful or event-making. Jefferson wished to be remembered after he was gone as "the author of the Declaration of Independence, the statute of Virginia for religious liberty, and father of the University of Virginia." Yet separately or together these achievements do not indicate that he was an eventful or event-making man. There is much in the contemporary rhetoric of democracy which would now be different had Jefferson not composed the Declaration of Independence, but the vision and faith to which he gave such felicitous phrasing were common to the distinguished company of whom he was one. The Statute on Religious Freedom gave formal expression to a movement of religious toleration already making its way through the states. The future of higher education in America, which already had a distinguished past before Jefferson, could hardly be said to have been profoundly influenced by him.

Oddly enough, from the point of view of narrow historical action, it is to something by which Jefferson himself set much less store that we must turn to find evidence for his event-making status. This is the Louisiana Purchase, in which he was the moving figure. He carried it through in the teeth of an opposition strong enough to have daunted a weaker man. And yet had this territory not been acquired from Napoleon when it was, England would probably have fallen heir to it at the Congress of Vienna if not sooner. Without the Louisiana territory—and the west to which it furnished access—the United States might have remained an Atlantic seaboard power. Its political history as well as its economic history might have been very different. There is no assurance that another incumbent of the presidency than Jefferson would have had the foresight and energy required to seize this golden opportunity to remove a foreign power and potential enemy from our borders, and at the same time to double the area under the American flag. But however we evaluate Jefferson's part in the territorial expansion of the United States, his stature as a man and thinker and his role as a historical force on American culture do not depend upon it. There is room for others besides those whom we call historical "heroes" in a democracy.[1]

What shall we say of historical figures who enjoyed great political power and whose reigns, although outwardly uneventful, seem to be conspicuous for their peace and prosperity? This is the type of situation with which Wood was primarily concerned, and which he too easily set down to the credit of the ruling individuals. When can they be credited with it and when not? And if they are credited with it, when can they be regarded as eventful or event-making? Our illustration here will be drawn from a period that might be called "the golden age" of Roman history.

Gibbon gives it as a considered judgment that after the reign of Augustus the happiness of all the European peoples "depended on the character of a single man"— that is, on whoever happened to be the Roman Emperor. In an agricultural society, where people could find refuge and a living in the interstices of the economy, this could hardly have been the case. But in view of the immense powers for good or evil wielded by the Roman Emperors, we can appreciate the truth behind Gibbon's exaggeration. Yet historically, the most uneventful period of the Roman Empire from the point of view of wars, rebellions, palace revolutions, incursions of barbarians, was the forty-two-year reign of the two Antonines, Pius and Marcus, in the second century of the Christian era. Of their united reigns Gibbon writes with positively un-English enthusiasm and unrestraint. They

[1] *Cf.* Chapter Eleven below on "The Hero and Democracy."

are "possibly the only period of history in which the
happiness of a great people was the sole object of government." And not merely the object of government
but the result! In one of the most extreme statements
ever penned by any historian of note he asserts: "If a
man were called to fix the period in the history of the
world, during which the condition of the human race
was most happy and prosperous, he would, without hesi-
tation, name that which elapsed from the death of Domitian to the accession of Commodus." [1]

A truly remarkable—and uneventful—period! At first
glance it appears that our categories do not apply to it.
Where nothing or little happens there is no call for
eventful or event-making men. Yet we cannot resist the
feeling that if only a tithe of what Gibbon says of them
is true, the Antonines are historically just as significant
as the Emperors who extended the boundaries of Rome,
codified its laws, or altered its religion. But to be justified
this feeling must rest on the belief, tacitly assumed by
Gibbon, that the order, tranquillity, and prosperity of
an era are the *consequences of policies* adopted by these
absolute rulers during their reign. That is to say, they
prevented dire events that otherwise would have occurred. Certainly, if we hold the Roman Emperors responsible for the "crimes, follies and misfortunes" of

---

[1] *Op. cit.*, vol. I, p. 70. It is in this connection that his famous re-
mark about history was made. Of the first Antonine he tells us: "His
reign is marked by the rare advantage of furnishing very few materials for history: which is, indeed, little more than the register of the
crimes, follies and misfortunes of mankind." As a historian Gibbon
himself did not live up to this gloomy conception of history, *i.e.*, his
history registers much more.

their reigns, as Gibbon does, we must credit them for the peace, wisdom, and good fortune, too, even if their lives do not make as interesting reading as those of Nero, Caligula, and Commodus.

Whether the Roman Emperors were in fact responsible for the condition of the country to the extent assumed by Gibbon, who was unconsciously much addicted to the heroic interpretation of history, is highly disputable. Later historians are convinced that the state of Roman agriculture accounts for much more about Roman history and the happiness of its people than the character of the Roman Emperors. But this is hardly the place to settle the question. The main point is that the outwardly uneventful appearance of a period—its prosperity—is either the consequence of a policy adopted by the ruling individuals, or the consequence of social and economic conditions (together with other factors) whose development has not been appreciably influenced by policy. In the first case, those who are responsible for the policy may be eventful or event-making men depending upon what an analysis of the situation reveals. In the second case, the historical phenomenon can be adequately explained without introducing heroes in any of the senses previously considered. To the extent that political action can influence the prosperity of an era, the Antonines may have been largely responsible, as Gibbon believes, for this happy interlude in Roman history. But the prosperity of an era is never by itself sufficient evidence to warrant an inference about existing political leadership. No historian could reasonably maintain that we owe the postwar years of prosperity in the United States to the leadership of Harding and Coolidge.

The eventful man is a creature of events in that by a happy or unhappy conjunction of circumstances he finds himself in a position where action or abstention from action is decisive in a great issue. But he need not be aware of that issue and how his action or inaction affects it. The members of the Committee of Public Safety during the French Revolution were, as a group, eventful men. But only Robespierre and St. Just were event-making in that they realized above all others what was at stake after Louis XVI had been deposed. Napoleon believed that if Robespierre had remained in power, France would have settled down to orderly processes of republican government and made Napoleon's accession to power impossible. But Robespierre was the architect of his own downfall and, despite all the politically motivated efforts to rehabilitate him, of the downfall of Republican France. Together with St. Just, he is responsible for carrying the Terror *beyond* the interests of national defense and public safety.[1]

Although Robespierre disapproved of the more barbaric excesses of indiscriminate executions and juridical

---

[1] Seven out of every ten persons guillotined or shot during the French terror were workers, peasants, and members of the lower middle class. The most recent studies show that of the approximately 17,000 victims, *i.e.*, those sentenced after "trial," not counting those shot out of hand or those among the 500,000 political prisoners who succumbed to horrible prison conditions, 31¼ per cent were workers, 28 per cent peasants, and 10½ per cent belonged to the lower middle class. See Donald Greer, *The Incidence of the Terror during the French Revolution: A Statistical Interpretation,* p. 166, Cambridge, 1935.

frame-ups, it was his own policy that prepared the way for them. The Terror, to the point that Robespierre approved it, did not save France from the flames of counterrevolution. It supplied fuel to those flames. By terrorizing tens of thousands of Frenchmen who were genuinely hostile to despotism, it made easier Napoleon's usurpation. An incidental distinction of Robespierre is that by charging his opponents, even when they were as far apart as Danton and Anarchisis Cloots, with being spies in English pay, he set a fashion that was to be followed in the Russian Revolution. It was bad enough that Robespierre proclaimed: "The Republic owes its enemies nothing but death." It was historically fatal when he began to regard the enemies of Robespierre as the enemies of the Republic.

The disproportion between the ordinary capacities which the eventful man brings to history and the extraordinary effects of his actions is best illustrated by the personality of the Emperor Justinian and the place he fills in history. The great military achievements under his reign, won by Belisarius, the codification of Roman law, the closing of the philosophic schools at Athens, his intervention in theological affairs, his vast architectural works, had a profound influence on European culture. But at no point did Justinian rise above the level of mediocrity. Although he made the decisions that moved much abler men than himself into action, he showed no clear purpose in what he was doing or any conception of the effects his decisions would have on what he thought he was doing.

Justinian's most eventful act, according to Fisher, was the destruction of the heretical Arian Goths in Italy in the middle of the sixth century and the resulting desolation of the whole Italian peninsula. The rulers of the Goths had pursued a policy of strict religious tolerance toward the orthodox Christians in their realm. When Justinian ordered his generals to take the field against them, the Goths sued for peace again and again with offers of tribute and perpetual vassaldom. But the bigoted Justinian was adamant. Theodora, his beautiful, influential, and much wiser spouse, might have prevailed upon him to call off his generals, as she frequently did on other occasions, but for reasons of state she was more interested in protecting a different variety of heresy. The Goths were ultimately exterminated root and branch. "It was a profound error to destroy them. Had they been left in peace there might have been no Lombard invasions, no papal state, no revival of the Empire in the West, and the political unity which Italy so painfully achieved in the reign of Queen Victoria might have been realized in the reign of Ethelbert." [1]

Whether this event should be called an "error" depends, of course, on one's religious predilections. Those who accept the theology of the Council of Nicea call Justinian's crusade a blessing. But error or blessing, the act was fateful for the history of Europe.

*   *   *   *

At this point it is necessary to consider the relation between the hero and social interests. For one way of

[1] Fisher, *op. cit.*, vol. I., p. 131.

losing sight of the problem is to show that heroic action fits into the needs of a class already in power or of a class that comes into power after his work is done. Such an analysis, even when it is true, does not rule out the possibility that the class that remains in power and the class that comes to power do so in virtue of the unique qualities of the hero who serves their interests. But very often it is assumed that this possibility has been ruled out when all that has been established is that the hero must take note of social interests and find support among them.

The event-making figure in history obviously can achieve nothing by himself alone. He is dependent upon a narrow group of lieutenants or assistants who constitute a "machine," and upon a much broader group in the population whom we may call a social class. Both groups are tied to him by bonds of interest, but the nature of the interests is different. An oversimplified conception of the role of interests often presents the event-making figure as their servant, selected because of his capacity to further them and replaceable when he fails. The event-making figure is thus reduced once more to an instrument of a historical or class Purpose, that is, the purposes of other men. The effect of his own purpose is regarded as a minor detail. That many, if not most, of the political personalities who stride the boards of history for a brief moment are instruments of other people's purposes may be granted. But it cannot be granted for those whom we have called event-making figures. We shall consider the relation of the hero, first to the social class that supports him, and then turn to his machine.

The dependence of the eventful figure on the support of a social class is much more in evidence before he accedes to power than when he is in possession of power and commands the state forces of coercion and education. A powerful social class which sees its vested position threatened, or which desires to use political power to break the vested position of another class, can usually arrange to give a candidate for the role of hero the *chance* to make good. But he may not be able to carry out all the tasks entrusted to him. His role may be that of a Bruening, a Schleicher, a von Papen, a Hoover, a Kerensky, or even a Leon Blum. But when he does make good, his very success, if he is skillful enough, makes him independent of the class chiefly responsible for his selection. He may still serve its interests, but the decision to do so is his now and not theirs.

The independence of the event-making man, over and against the class whose interest he actually or presumably has been selected to serve, is achieved in various ways. First, he can build up other social interests in opposition to the class that has sponsored him. This is not difficult because in the demagogic preparation for power he has already promised much to other classes, except the national scapegoat. Since he always speaks in the name of the nation or people, he can justify his independence of the class that has originally supported him in terms of the very myths this class has helped to propagate. Secondly, the event-making man comes into control of the armed forces of the state. Not infrequently he already enjoys some military prestige and power before his advent to power. Third, he brings his machine into play to take over and administer social functions, pulverize opposition, and consolidate military influence. As far as possible the machine reduces all potential centers of resistance and draws into its periphery all independent institutions. In fact, it is the machine that makes possible the pursuit of the first two methods by which the event-making figure emancipates himself from dependence upon the class whose social need gave him his original opportunity.

It is to the machine then and not to the social class that we must look to uncover the chief dependence of the hero. Whether it be a political party, a Jesuit religious order, a military camarilla, the hero must bind it to himself with hoops stronger than steel. If he is to play the man of the hour and pay his debts to the social class that supported him, the machine is a convenient instrument. If he decides to take a course independent from the one he was expected to follow, its iron loyalty is all the more necessary. In either case the machine must become *his* machine if he is to triumph. How is this accomplished? In the main by giving its members certain material and psychological privileges that are sufficiently distinctive to mark them off as a separate social grouping. As a group they must be convinced that they are the senior partner in any political alliance with other social groups. They either supplant the existing bureaucracy or fuse with it in such a way that they occupy all the strategic posts.

The historical hero, however, cannot become merely

the instrument of his machine and enjoy power long. For all his reliance upon it, he must remain its master. This he accomplishes by making it evident that he is indispensable to the continuation of its privileges, that his downfall is their downfall, but not necessarily that its downfall is his. Just as he uses the machine to bring other social groups in line, the hero uses these social groups, tamed but resentful over the privileges lost to the machine, to keep the latter in tow. The event-making figure in history wins the opportunity to move freely by skillfully playing off against each other the groups upon whom he is dependent. That is why he is more than an instrument of a social class and more than a captain of a robber band. That is why he can be ruthless, if necessary, to the social class whose interests he claims to represent. That is why he can whirl his machine around into an abrupt spin in an opposite direction without consulting them or fearing defection. It goes without saying that he always strives to keep his machine in order, free of the grit and sand of dissidence and with an ample supply of spare parts at hand for necessary replacements.

Our conclusion then is that without meeting some social and group interests—economic, national, psychological—the hero cannot influence historical events; but he meets them in such a way that he always retains a considerable degree of freedom in choosing which interests to further and which to suppress or weaken. The behavior of most historical figures in relation to political and social issues can be explained in terms of the interests that speak through them. But there are individuals in history who not only talk back but react in such a way as to modify the original relations of social interest in a radical way.

The particular role that any historical character plays in relation to social interests may not be apparent from what he says about himself. He may claim to be serving the interests of a class when he is actually doing something quite different, or he may regard himself as completely independent of all social pressures when in fact he is merely a servant, sometimes even a contemptible tool, of special privilege.

This raises the question of individual consciousness and historical action.

*   *   *   *

Many leading historical figures have little consciousness, or a false consciousness, of the eventful place they hold in history. What they do seems to them to be exacted by the necessities of the situation, working through them to a foreordained result, rather than achieved by voluntary action and intelligent planning in whose absence affairs would turn out quite differently. Even genuine event-making men, like Cromwell and Lenin, regarded themselves respectively as instruments of divine and dialectical necessity.

On the other hand, there are historical characters, borne along on the tide of events, who feel that they are controlling the direction of the wave. Or they make claims of having influenced events in one field whereas their real influence is in another. A particularly instructive example of this was the pathetic illusion of Neville Chamberlain that it was he alone who was settling the destiny of our century.

Immediately after the Munich Pact in 1938, Chamberlain was widely regarded as an event-making man, admired by those who approved of his policy and condemned by those who did not. The former agreed with his conviction that he had snatched "peace for our time" from the very jaws of the Moloch of war. The latter were convinced that after Munich no western power would or could dispute Hitler's march to the East. A few made a more sober estimate of the situation.

Although we know that the Munich Pact did not bring peace in our time, its actual historical significance is still shrouded in obscurity. It depends upon the answer to the following questions. What would have happened if Chamberlain and Daladier, who dragged after him in reluctant tow, had presented an ultimatum of war to Hitler instead of flying to Munich and coming to terms with him? Would Hitler have marched into the Sudetenland as he later marched into Poland, despite the fact that Russia had not yet assured him that he would have no second front? If he had, would the English and French have been able in the ensuing war to put up a better defense than they did when war came a year later? Was the Czech military strength of greater value than a year won for additional armament—inadequate as the latter was even in 1939? Would a war begun in 1938 have resulted in the overrunning of England before the United States, still largely peace-minded, could enter it? Had war broken out, would the large pacifist and isolationist groups in England and America have seen through the hypocrisy of Hitler's claims in behalf of the "poor Sudetens" who indisputably were more German than Czech?

Without more data at our command we cannot answer these questions. But we can answer the question whether or not Chamberlain's capitulation was merely a strategic postponement, forced by lack of preparedness, of the inescapable showdown. This is a matter that is not shrouded in obscurity. If it were true, as some of his defenders have urged, that this is what determined Chamberlain's historic decision, Chamberlain's stature as a statesman would be enormously increased. If it were true, and if the Axis goes down to defeat, historians might very well regard him as among the greatest event-making men of his generation. But it is not true. By his unwearied insistence that the peace had been saved, Chamberlain himself provides the evidence that his decision was not motivated by the desire to gain time for preparation. Even if it turns out that the year won by Munich was necessary to eventual victory, Chamberlain did not organize or plan it that way. In the light of the most favorable outcome, he was not the contriver of good fortune but, duped by his fears and made foolish by his self-righteousness, he was at best a happy accident in that good fortune. His judgment was a thousand times wrong even if historians of a later day, writing in a free world, might congratulate themselves on the lucky fact that, by gaining a year's grace in 1938, England was able to stave off France's fate in 1940. At best, then, Chamberlain may be considered an eventful man, certainly not event-making.

How fantastically false was Chamberlain's consciousness of his own historical role may be plainly seen in his memorable address to the House of Commons on October 6, 1938. He unequivocally declared that whether there should be war or not depended upon him, and on him alone, and that his decision had banished its shadows for our time.

> Anyone who had been through what I have had to go through, day after day and face to face, with the thought that in the last resort it would be I, I alone, who would have to say that "yes" or "no" which would decide the fate of millions of my countrymen and their wives and families—anyone who has been through that, would not readily forget. . . . A man who gets to my age in my position tends to feel that he may disregard any abuse that is levelled at him if his conscience approves what he has done. Looking back on those events I feel convinced . . . that my action was only what one in my position would do. I say that by my action I did avert war.

It is a sobering thought that a statesman in a democracy can believe and openly proclaim that on his single word the destiny of his nation depends. But far more significant here is Chamberlain's political innocence in seriously entertaining the notion that he could stop a war that had been in the making from the very moment Hitler assumed power.

Once Fascism had consolidated its internal position, it was beyond the effort of a host of peace-loving statesmen to block the dynamic force to war that was generated by a peculiar combination of economic need, fanatical ideology, and intense chauvinism. Hitler made no secret of his intentions before he came to power, and every step he took after he came to power showed that German society was being geared to total war. The sole effect of negotiation with him could be at most a calendar victory—an enforced change in his timetable. This might have tremendous importance, but only in relation to the striking power of the armies when war broke out. A statesman who imagined that, by a pact or memorandum, or by any concession short of total capitulation, he could immobilize the tensions straining toward release betrayed the perspectives of a small-town politician.

There are situations in the world no hero can master. They break with such fury that neither the potentially event-making man nor his pedestrian camp follower can withstand it, although they may ride them out differently. These situations are commonly found at the end of prolonged periods of distress and oppression, as in the great revolutionary upheavals. They are also found when two powerful nations are so organized that one or both cannot feel safe so long as the main trade routes, the markets reached by them, and the sources of raw materials and supply are straddled by the other—conditions antecedent to many wars from the days when Rome faced Carthage to the days when Imperial Germany challenged British sea power and Japan strove for the hegemony of the entire Pacific. In general, whenever opposing sets of interests are conceived in an absolute way so that the fulfillment of one set demands the liquidation of the other, without compromise or pity or reference to other interests that are common, we have the makings of social catastrophes. They burst on society with the elemental force of natural phenomena and overwhelm alike the just and the unjust, the wise and the foolish.

But there are other situations in which a gifted man of good or evil genius can so profoundly affect men and events that he becomes an event-making man. That there are such situations and such men is something difficult to establish. In the next chapter we shall examine a great historical event as a crucial test of the theoretical position already sketched. We will show that there has been at least one event-making man in our time who has redetermined the course of history and, in so doing, has influenced the life of the great majority of men, women, and children on the face of the globe.

* * * *

Before proceeding to the evidence that there has been at least one event-making man in our own times, something should be said about the role of women in history. So far we have been discussing in the main eventful and event-making men in history. What of the position of women? Does history show any indisputably eventful or event-making women? They are always around, but to what extent do they count in determining the world's affairs?

The four women for whom the largest claims have been made are Cleopatra, Theodora, Madame de Pompadour, and Catherine II of Russia.[1]

Cleopatra is the most legendary of all the eventful women of history. But her influence on affairs has been enormously exaggerated, and she herself has been the subject of romantic myths that are great poetry but poor history. Ever since Pascal's brief comment on her in his *Pensées,* she has become the perennial illustration of the way in which the history of the world depends upon trifling details. "Cleopatra's nose, had it been shorter, the whole aspect of the world would have been different." Pascal's words have stimulated important reflections on the nature of history, but the example he took was unfortunate. It seems a pity to destroy a pretty story, but the true story is perhaps just as interesting.

A judicious evaluation of what we know about Cleopatra and her times makes it clear that her nose had little to do with her influence on the younger Pompey, Caesar, and Antony. What is more important, her influence on them had very little effect upon the history of the world. She made a great difference to Antony's life, but little to the history of the Roman Empire. Caesar would have triumphed over Pompey in any event; Octavian and Antony would have had to settle the question of succession to the

[1] Since we have already considered Madame de Pompadour in our criticism of Plechanov, we shall say no more about her.

mantle of Caesar, and the odds of victory were with the former even if the latter had been immune to Cleopatra's charms. What brought the great Romans to Egypt were the exigencies of political warfare together with the necessity of ensuring that this Nile-blessed country would remain the granary of Italy, then in the process of acute agricultural decline. While in Egypt they naturally improved on their opportunity, but the history of Rome would have been substantially the same if there had never been a Cleopatra.

Like most women who have played some role in history, Cleopatra's influence was achieved by influencing men. And like most women who have influenced eventful men, Cleopatra owed her success not so much to her beauty as to qualities of intelligence, will, personality, and an obscure appeal that does not depend upon face or figure. She seems to have been petite and daintily built, but Plutarch tells us that Octavia, Antony's wife, whom Antony deserted for Cleopatra, compared favorably to her both in youth and beauty. From the available accounts, even if Cleopatra's nose had been shorter, she would have been no less irresistible, since the change would have been more in harmony with her pert spirit.[1] Pascal's famous question is thus answered in respect to her influence on men. But suppose she had been a fright,

[1] "For her actual beauty was not in itself so remarkable that none could be compared with her, or that no one could see her without being struck by it, but the contact of her presence, if you lived with her, was irresistible: The attraction of her person, joining with the charm of her conversation, and the character that attended all she said or did, was something bewitching."—Plutarch.

would world history have been very different? It is
hardly likely.

Cleopatra was not a great courtesan but a shrewd politician, with overreaching ambitions, who fought a losing
battle to preserve the independence of her empire. The
preservation of her empire was the fixed principle of
her policy, to which she showed a far greater constancy
than to any of her royal lovers. She was willing to learn
to love anybody who would save her dynasty. She threw
Antony over and tricked him into suicide after the battle
of Actium and would have added Octavian to her collec-
tion if his temperament had not been so cold. Ferrero and
other historians suggest that she inspired Julius Caesar to
dream of a World Empire with her beside him as Queen
of the Earth, but it is unlikely that Caesar's ambition ever
waited upon anything but opportunity. Cleopatra was
Caesar's personal weakness, not his political mentor:
Caesar was Cleopatra's political patron, hardly her romantic ideal. At any rate, the men who killed Caesar and
who were very well acquainted with his affairs and the
influences to which he was subjected made no attempt
to molest Cleopatra, who was living with Caesar in Rome
at the time of his death. Had she inspired him with the
ambition to become Emperor of the Roman world, it is
extremely unlikely that they would have taken no action
against her.

As in the case of Cleopatra, most of what we know
about the Empress Theodora is derived from sources that
are hostile or unsympathetic. Even after discounting the
malice of religious fanatics whose orthodoxy she out-

raged, there is no reason to doubt the main facts of her early life. She was born to a family of circus performers, and she herself became a professional dancer and actress. In Byzantium this was the badge of another profession as well. Before she reached the age of twenty she had become the most notorious figure both on and off the stage in virtue of her scandalous performances and the multiplicity of her lovers. After a period in the provinces she underwent a religious conversion and returned to Constantinople where she lived in obscurity. How she met the Emperor Justinian, who was already quite mature at the time, is not known, but his passion for her was so great and pure that he violated all precedent and made her Empress in A.D. 527. She seems to have lived an exemplary domestic life with him and to have devoted herself to good works. The redemption of fallen women was one of her chief concerns. It is said that she caused the laws on marriage and divorce to be strengthened in favor of women, was an energetic matchmaker, and encouraged ill-treated and unhappily married wives to seek redress and consolation elsewhere. On the whole, she had a very poor opinion of men with the exception of the adoring Justinian whom she regarded as something of a fool.

Theodora's historical significance lies in the power she wielded. There was apparently nothing she could not get the doting Justinian to do. She mothered and warmly defended grave heretical doctrines in an age of ruthless fanaticism, fought for the rights of dissenters, deposed one Pope and made another a servant of her will—all this despite the orthodox professing Justinian—gave orders to the military, intrigued with subordinates, appointed and removed the highest officers of the realm, saved Justinian's throne from a rebellion. In short, she showed herself the keenest statesman in the whole line of Byzantine rulers. As a woman she was attractive, but her contemporaries thought her more graceful than beautiful and were most impressed by her spirit, intelligence, and sharp wit. Only Justinian thought her perfect. "Upon the most momentous questions Justinian was pleased to take the advice of 'the most reverend spouse whom God had given unto him' whom he loved to call 'his sweetest delight.' "[1]

Nonetheless, despite her enormous power, Theodora at most must be regarded as a potentially event-making woman. The heresies she defended made little headway after her death. The Imperial treasury was bankrupted by fantastic extravagances. Had she applied the habits of a thrifty housewife to the royal economy her influence would have been more lasting. The Empire of Justinian crumbled in the west, and became weaker and weaker before the onslaughts of the eastern "barbarians." Theodora was in a position where she undoubtedly could have influenced Justinian to forego the reconquest of the western countries. Had she done so the Papacy would probably have played a very different role in western Europe. Only in what she could have done but failed to do can she be regarded as event-making. All of her posi-

[1] C. Diehl, *Byzantine Portraits*, English translation, p. 64, New York, 1927.

tive achievements had little consequence for subsequent history.

Among modern eventful women, probably of greatest distinction is Catharine II, that "Russian Empress of German blood and French culture." It is difficult to evaluate her influence since she was a contemporary of other eventful monarchs like Frederick II, and because the groundswell of bourgeois revolution had already begun in the west. But by any reckoning, those accomplishments for which she was chiefly responsible were very impressive. Through her efforts, Russia acquired a full-fledged and permanent influence on the political history of western Europe. No longer could she be ignored in the affairs of the more developed nations. Karl Marx once declared that Russia was the most reactionary political influence on revolutionary developments in western Europe during the entire nineteenth century—an influence which was the continuation of Catherine's policy. Under Catherine, Russia tremendously expanded its national boundaries. She added an area of almost 250,000 square miles to Russian domains. At the same time, despite her enlightened ideas, Catherine riveted the chains of serfdom more securely on the Russian masses and retarded the development of progressive social forces for generations. With great political acumen she secularized church property and tied the Russian church to the crown so closely that from then on it became primarily an instrument of dynastic rule.

However we appraise them, these were no inconsiderable achievements. In virtue of what qualities was she

able to bring them off? Certainly not by her beauty or
other feminine charms. She was not beautiful enough to
hold her own husband whom she deposed and murdered
in order to clear the way for herself. And although she
never denied the needs of her passionate nature, she did
not permit any of her favorites to swerve her from her
fixed policy, the consolidation of a powerful national
state pursuing an independent course exclusively for its
own interests. To carry out this policy successfully required outstanding political talent, particularly on the
part of a foreigner who had entered Russia as a royal no-
body, usurped the throne, and had to hold it against a
succession of pretenders. Such talent Catherine possessed
to an extraordinary degree. She numbered some able men
among her advisers and lieutenants, but they were completely subordinate to her purposes. Despite her amours
there were no male de Pompadours in her entourage.
Her eventfulness as a historic character was due to
unique gifts of political intelligence.

It should be noted, however, that, as far as her domestic rule is concerned, at no point did she run counter
to the interests of the large feudal landholders. There is
no reason to doubt her early sincerity in espousing the
ideas of Montesquieu, Beccaria, and the French Encyclo-
pedists. Her abandonment of progressive social ideals
was to some extent the result of her realization that there
was no social class in Russia strong enough to support
economic reforms that would have imperiled the position
of the large landholders. Since she could not change the
status quo, she decided to strengthen it at the cost of the

peasants. Without her the emancipation of the serfs would probably have come sooner. But limited as her freedom of action was, she seems to have been an event-making woman, "every inch a 'political being' unmatched by anyone of her sex in modern history." [1]

[1] Hotzsch, in *The Cambridge Modern History*, vol. VI, p. 701.

X *The Russian Revolution: A Test Case*

THE THESIS of this chapter is that had it not been for the work of one man we should be living in a vastly different world today.

There are four stages to the argument. The first is that, next to the first World War, the most momentous occurrence of the twentieth century has been the Russian Revolution of October 1917. By "most momentous" we mean that it has had a greater influence on the political, social, and economic history of the world since its occurrence than any other single event. The second step in the argument is that the Russian Revolution was not inevitable. The third is that it was triumphant because of the directing leadership of Lenin and that without him it would have been lost. The fourth is that if the Russian Revolution had not taken place the cultural, political, and, in part, the economic life of the world would have been very different.

184

1

The Russian Revolution of February 1917 which destroyed Czarism and moved toward the introduction of democratic political forms on the western model was unplanned but historically expected. The October Revolution of 1917, which destroyed political democracy and substituted a minority party dictatorship in its stead, was planned but historically unexpected.

This seeming paradox is easily explained. Whereas all political groups, except pensioners of the court and other reactionary elements, anticipated the downfall of the autocracy through a "February" Revolution at almost any moment after the outbreak of the Russo-Japanese War, no one dreamed of an "October" Revolution as a *realistic possibility* as late as ten months before its actual occurrence. This goes without saying for those who were later to oppose the October Revolution. But not even the Bolsheviks themselves, who carried out the Revolution and who were committed to a belief in the historical inevitability of proletarian dictatorship, had any inkling that their chance would come so soon. Their belief in proletarian dictatorship was a theoretical and programmatic commitment—part of a doctrine conceived to be universally valid as the goal of an international movement whose ultimate objective was world socialism. The grand political strategy, as distinct from tactical maneuvers, was to be followed not only in Russia but elsewhere as well. Not even the most extreme party doctrinaires regarded the conquest of state power in Russia, a short ten months before they took it, as a serious item on the agenda of history.

If any evidence of this were needed, we could cite the expectation of the Bolshevik leaders that the socialist revolution would occur first in the highly industrialized countries of the west. At best they hoped that a democratic revolution in Russia would set off a socialist revolution in the west which in time would swing Russia, too, into the same orbit. More important still, in an address delivered before a group of young Swiss socialists shortly before he returned to Russia, Lenin himself indicated that he did not anticipate an "October" revolution in his own lifetime. The notion that a socialist state could exist for any length of time in Russia, as an island in a capitalist world, would have been laughed off as a fantasy if anyone had suggested it.

What were the consequences of the Russian Revolution? We shall pass no judgment on their desirability but shall restrict ourselves to uncovering the objective connections between events.

The first result was to prolong somewhat the duration of the First World War by removing Germany's second front. Although the influence of the Russian example and of revolutionary agitation softened the German home front, the decision of the Imperial High Command to sue for peace was a military one. After the German Spring offensive in 1918, made possible by the transfer of troops from the east, had collapsed, victory for German arms was no longer possible.

Not so immediate but perhaps more far-reaching in

its effects was the withdrawal of one-sixth of the world's surface from the international economy. With absolute monopolistic control over foreign trade, introduced almost at once by the Bolsheviks, the competitive market was destroyed. Not only was the importation of commodities prohibited but the policy of the government and the reluctance of foreign investors to risk their funds because of prior repudiation, both natural under the circumstances, cut off the importation of capital. This tendency, initiated under Lenin to prevent capitalist restoration, became strengthened under Stalin when the construction of "Socialism in one country" became the standing order of the day. The full effects of Russia's withdrawal from the world market were apparent in the devastating crisis of 1929-1932 when huge surpluses of commodities and capital piled up in the chief capitalist countries for lack of outlets while unemployment and want mounted correspondingly. The potential Russian market could have absorbed a vast amount of goods and services. Its closed doors accentuated the severity of the crisis.

When the Bolsheviks took power, they did not expect to hold it without a revolution in the west. Once that revolution took place, they assumed that Russia, because of the primitive state of its productive forces, would lapse once more into its backward role in a socialist world economy. To facilitate the "inevitable" revolution in the west, the Communist International was founded. It was distinguished then and forever afterward from the Soviet regime and the Bolshevik Party only by a different letterhead for its stationery.

The "inevitable," however, did not occur. The few efforts made to force it in Germany, Hungary, Finland, and China resulted in disaster. The Bolsheviks had to hold on or voluntarily abandon state power. Marx's doctrine that no ruling class ever voluntarily surrenders its power turned out to be true for the dictatorship of the Bolshevik Party, too. The reversal in the policy of the Communist International was signaled by Stalin who had succeeded to Lenin's mantle, despite the latter's political testament. From then on "the defense of the Soviet Union" became transformed from a slogan, which had rallied the western workers during the years of Allied intervention, into the guiding principle behind the activities of Communists throughout the world. The history of every national Communist Party is proof of this. For example, the French Communist Party which bitterly opposed the present war changed its line not when its *own* country was invaded by Hitler but only after Russia was invaded. The same holds true everywhere else.

The defense of the Soviet Union was now identified with the stability of the Bolshevik regime. The stability of the regime was bound up with correct relations with other states, particularly the absence of international conflict. These good relations could easily be imperiled if revolutionary movements, which derived their material resources in part and their ideal inspiration entire from the Bolshevik regime, were to make a bid for power and fail. The ensuing struggle and reaction might unloose the much-dreaded war and intervention which would interrupt the building up of "socialism." Consequently, the Soviet rulers, because of the needs of national defense and of the expansion of the state economy, developed a vested interest in preserving peace. What is more, they committed themselves to maintaining the domestic status quo in all capitalist countries insofar as its upset might provoke international conflict. Where the Soviet government believed it had nothing to fear in the way of interventionist designs by a foreign country, or believed it could turn these designs aside by trade or political treaty, it was eager to enter into cordial relations with that country, whether it was totalitarian Italy and Turkey or democratic France and England. If anything, because of the history of the early years, it was more suspicious of the latter than of the former. Even after the advent of Fascism in Germany, despite Hitler's candid declaration of his policy toward Russia, the Bolshevik regime was punctilious in fulfilling all its treaties, pacts, and trade agreements. In fact, it renewed the old ones and entered into new ones with Hitler, not because it had no fear of his intentions but in order to avoid a provocation that Hitler's words and acts showed he would not wait upon.

At the same time that it acquired a vested interest in the perpetuation of the status quo in foreign countries, the Bolshevik regime was compelled to keep national Communist Parties alive within them. *It was an axiom of Bolshevik doctrine that the differences between any group of capitalist powers was as nothing compared to the differences between the Soviet Union and all capit-*

alist powers. The palpable contrasts between capitalist democracies and Fascist countries were regarded as superficial. Fascism itself was defined as the final and normal phase of democratic development in the era of finance capitalism. It followed, according to Bolshevik doctrine, that there was an ever-present peril that any or all capitalist countries might attack the Soviet Union instead of one another. To forestall such a dire eventuality, and to secure active, strategically situated allies in case it did occur, the national Communist Parties had to be strengthened as an elementary form of insurance. As the Bolsheviks conceived it, this meant that they had to achieve leadership and domination in the socialist and labor movements of all countries, not to carry out a revolution, but to influence the national and foreign policy of those countries, directly and indirectly, as the interests of the Soviet Union required. To do this they had to eliminate or subordinate to themselves all other socialist, labor, and even democratic liberal groups.

The greatest triumphs enjoyed by the Bolsheviks outside of Russia were not the overthrow of any capitalist state but the destruction of working-class and socialist unity in all countries where affiliated sections of the Communist International could gain a foothold. Sometimes this was accomplished by boring from within and the well-known Trojan-horse tactics; sometimes by open splits and organization of parallel political parties and trade unions; sometimes by both. The net effect was the weakening of powers of resistance to forces of domestic reaction, particularly to the large industrialists and land-owners as well as the dispossessed middle classes subject to growing Fascist influence, who were uncompromis-ingly hostile to the Soviet Union.

In this connection the cases of Italy and Germany are particularly instructive, for they reflect two stages in the influence of the Bolshevik regime on the working class of the west.

While Lenin was still alive the Bolsheviks hoped to force the "inevitable" birth of proletarian dictatorships in the west. But to force it, they had to take leadership. In doing so they abandoned the remarkable tactical flexi-bility they showed on their home ground and laid down dogmatic prescriptions for action in all other countries based on their own historical experience. This meant smashing existing socialist movements that had other policies and approaches. In Italy, the powerful and mili-tant Italian Socialist Party was disorganized and split by the Communist International at the very time when Mus-solini's cohorts, although still weak, were girding them-selves for a general offensive against labor and the Ital-ian democracy.

Lenin's strategy, however, both within Russia and without, especially in dealing with other working-class groups in relation to which the Bolsheviks were a minor-ity, all flowed from his conception of the nature of a revolutionary party. He could not have abandoned it without rejecting the cardinal principle of Bolshevism, *viz.*, the dictatorship of the Bolshevik Party over the proletariat as a condition precedent for the dictatorship of the proletariat.[1]

After the succession of revolutionary miscarriages in the west, the Bolsheviks turned toward the construction of socialism in Russia, transforming the Communist International into an instrument to achieve this aim. A revolution *now* in the capitalist countries would prove an embarrassment, even if it were peacefully achieved under non-Bolshevik auspices, because of the dangers of civil war, counterrevolution, and international conflict which it would provoke. In Germany from 1928 on, the Bolsheviks tricked themselves out with an ultrarevolutionary line but concentrated most of their energies in combatting other working-class parties. They declared that "the chief enemy" of genuine democracy and socialism was the German Socialist Party. They referred to its leaders and members as "Social-Fascists." On important occasions the German Communist Party co-operated with the Nazis in common action against the Weimar Republic. Even after Hitler's accession to power and the outlawing of the Communist Party, the Communist International denounced the German Socialist Party as "the chief enemy" of the working class.[2]

This line was changed in 1935 at the Seventh Congress of the Communist International when Hitler's will to war had become unmistakable even to the Kremlin. The new turn ushered in the period of the Popular Front.

[1] For an elaboration of this, see Chapters Seven and Eight in my *Reason, Social Myths and Democracy*, New York, 1940.
[2] Declaration of May 1, 1933.

The Popular Front was a Peace Front agitating for a collective security that would freeze the existing national boundaries of Europe and invoke sanctions against any country sending troops beyond its borders. The Popular Front was intended to embrace any group, independently of its social program, which accepted this program. In all Popular Fronts during this period the Communist Parties of the world were at the extreme right of the Coalition, arguing against any social changes that would imperil national unity. In France they sided with the Radical Socialists, who were conservative, against the Socialist Party. In England they called for a political coalition between the Liberal Party of Lloyd George and the English Labor Party. In Spain they were to the right of the Republicans and contested bitterly the social reforms proposed by the Socialists and Anarchists which would infringe on the rights of private property. The Communists, who yesterday had been ultrarevolutionary, today feared that even minor social reforms would create domestic opposition and chaos, strengthen Hitler, and drive democratic England and France into Hitler's camp. For the same reason, during this period there was an abatement of the struggle for colonial liberation by native Communist Parties in the English and French Empires.

In 1939 the line was switched once more when Stalin thought that, as a result of his pact with Hitler, the latter would go west and stay there. Again the "plutocratic western democracies" became the chief enemy, and war mongers to boot. Fascism was declared by the Kremlin to be merely a matter of political taste.

In 1941, Stalin perforce had to reverse himself once more, since Hitler gave him no alternative. The Bolshevik dogma, that all capitalist countries—and they still considered Germany a capitalist country—had more in common with one another than any one of them had with Russia, proved bankrupt. But at what cost!

It must be borne in mind that the Bolshevik campaign for domination over the international working-class movement and its liberal allies was not a piece of political diabolism on the part of Lenin and Stalin. It followed from the needs and interests of the world revolution and of the Soviet Union as Lenin and Stalin respectively interpreted them—needs and interests of which they considered themselves the *sole* spokesmen. Lenin reasoned that without the necessary knowledge and leadership, which the Bolsheviks alone possessed, revolutions were doomed. Stalin reasoned that, if the affiliated sections of the Comintern were to have any political weight in swaying the decisions of their government on matters that affected Russia, Bolshevik leadership of the masses in foreign countries was essential. Bolshevik leadership in both periods was disputed in most countries, partly because of the methods of rule or ruin by which it was sought, but mainly because socialists, trade unionists, and democrats refused to accept dictation on domestic issues by agents of a foreign power—one that despite its socialist appellation was unmistakably a dictatorship of a minority party over its proletariat and peasantry. But although the Bolsheviks did not succeed in achieving leadership, they succeeded brilliantly in fragmentizing the opposition to Fascism everywhere except in Austria where the clerical Fascists under Dollfuss and Schussnig took over that role.

Despite the fact that the Bolsheviks had abandoned the policy of world revolution for the preservation of peace, large sections of the conservative and propertied groups in western countries remained fearful of the Soviet power. The memory of the early years of the Russian Revolution had not died out. As the economic crisis deepened, they observed with acute discomfort the slow but definite increase of sentiment friendly to the Soviet Union among some sections of the workers, and even more so among the intellectuals of their own countries. The well-advertised increases in productive potentials during the Five-Year Plans exercised the influence of example upon those who, faced by declining living standards, preferred the promise of security to the bitter and uncertain bread of freedom. At home, restlessness, demonstrations, increasing tensions, and conflicts that became more acute as the curve of production went lower frightened the bankers, the industrialists, the landowners, and their political and ideological pensioners.

In Germany and Italy these were the groups which lifted Fascism into the saddle. For it cannot be too often repeated, neither Mussolini nor Hitler actually won power in open struggle. It was given them by influential conservative circles—"the best people"—who saw in Fascism the only alternative to Bolshevism. This sentiment was world-wide and accounted for the support Mussolini received not only in England but even in America. Thomas W. Lamont of the House of Morgan negotiated a loan that saved the Italian Fascist regime when it was tottering. Industrialists praised it: trains ran on time! Irving Babbitt, a leading member of the American professoriate, wrote: "Circumstances may arise when we may esteem ourselves fortunate if we get the American' equivalent of a Mussolini; he may be needed to save us from the American equivalent of a Lenin." [1] It is interesting to observe that these were the only social groups, aside from the outright organizational Fascists, who took seriously the agitational slogans of the Communist International—"either Communism or Fascism."

Undoubtedly much more influential than the possibility, fearful even if mythical, that the Bolsheviks would overrun the west were the economic decline of capitalism and its inability to come out of the throes of depression as quickly as it had in other periods. The sheer facts of unemployment and want compelled the existing governments to adopt measures that seemed to threaten the traditional position, prestige, and income of propertied conservative groups. These groups were prepared to let the crisis work itself out "normally," that is, at the cost of those who suffered most. They resented the taxes, the social welfare legislation, and all the halfway measures of regulated capitalism that sought to redistribute economic burdens without affecting the structure of the profit system.

[1] *Democracy and Leadership*, p. 312, New York, 1924.

The vigorous completion of the movement of social regulation which had begun in the Weimar Republic might have led to some variety of democratic socialism, but this was precluded by the increasing opposition of the industrialists and the Junkers, the crippling effects of the Versailles system, confusion of purpose and timidity on the part of the socialists, and the civil war in the labor movement which the Bolsheviks were waging with ever-growing intensity.

Into this situation, compounded of economic catastrophe and political ineptitude, the Fascists entered, bearing gifts and promises to all sections of the community. Harassed by the burden of social services, taxes, strikes, and the spectacle of miniature civil war on the streets of all large cities, the Hugenburgs, Thyssens, and Hindenburgs welcomed the Fascists so they might restore order "once and for all." After that was done, so they thought who had seen so many Chancellors come and go, the Fascists would either be sobered by the responsibility of rule or cashiered by the same mechanism through which they took over. The army at any rate would keep them within the bounds of sanity after the country had been "saved from Bolshevism." Once installed, however, the Fascists smashed the mechanism by which they came into power, politicalized the army, and harnessed the industrialists as well as their plants into an economy organized for total war.

After Hitler became Chancellor and ruler of Germany, matters moved rapidly toward the solution by force of the economic and political problems of Europe.

Just as Hitler's domestic policy was aided by conservative fear of Bolshevism, so his international policy, which aimed at the destruction of Russia as the first big step in the march toward world power, was aided by conservative and reactionary groups the world over. Conflicting national interests, of course, came into play. As a whole, conservatives in the west were friendlier to the Roman variety of totalitarianism than to the Nazi variety. But as a group they swung enough weight to prevent energetic action against Hitler until the hunted became strong enough to become the hunter.

It is often alleged that the calculated policy of the governing classes in France and England was to encourage Germany to march east at the expense of Poland, the Baltic States, and especially Russia. This thesis is offered in extenuation of the Soviet-Nazi Pact of 1939 which freed Hitler of his fear of a second front. It has little to recommend it. French distrust of Germany would never have been allayed by the sight of victorious German armies anywhere. But the decisive disproof of the allegations is the fact that both England and France declared war against Germany as soon as she marched due east to Russian borders. They did not do it, of course, to save Poland and Russia but to save themselves. Why did they wake up so late to the realization that Hitler threatened *them* and that they had to save themselves? Their false estimation of the nature of Fascism, their reluctance to forestall the rise of Hitler and the rearming of Germany, can be accounted for by the fear, not less influential because ungrounded, that the red flood of Bolshevism was the only possible alternative to the brown flood of Fascism. They were lamed in eye and mind and limb by the fear of Bolshevism, both before and after that unhappy day in January 1933 when Hindenburg betrayed the Weimar Republic. It was only when Hitler held the knife to the throat of Poland, and to Russia beyond her, that they realized that knife was intended for them, too.

Once Hitler made of Germany a Fascist state, the Second World War was only a matter of time. The world as we know it today, which a generation ago would have appeared as a Wellsian fantasy, became a historical reality.

In summary, then, of the first step of the argument: three chains of events radiating from the Russian Revolution converged to contribute strongly to the victory of Hitler:

a. The withdrawal of Russia from the world economy left a dead spot unable to absorb the flow of goods and services from other countries. This *accentuated* the economic crisis, which would have occurred anyhow, but in not so violent a form. It enabled Hitler to recruit his mass following from those who felt the impact of the crisis most sharply.

b. The destruction of the labor movement which, if it had been as unified as it was at the time of the monarchist Kapp putsch in Germany, could have stopped Fascism in it tracks or, at least, put up so strong a resistance that Germany would have been as exhausted as Spain.

c. The fear of Bolshevism and of the imposition of the Bolshevik pattern on the west. This led reactionary groups in Germany to call Hitler to power and explains the shortsighted indifference of reactionary groups in *other* capitalist countries to the rise of Fascism. Without the Russian Revolution, there would have been a Hitler movement anyway but it would not have triumphed. The worst alternative realizable in Germany would have been a period of reaction similar to other conservative swings of the past. But in time, unable to overcome the crisis endemic to capitalism, a conservative regime would have had to make way for German social democracy, instructed and strengthened by previous defeats, or it would have been compelled to pit itself against the overwhelming mass of the German people in open revolt.

2 and 3

However we assess the causal significance of the Russian Revolution for subsequent European development, we must face the position which asserts that the October Revolution was inevitable. The term "inevitable" in this connection is ambiguous. Even those who use it do not mean it literally. What they do mean is that, given its social and economic antecedents, the October Revolution was overwhelmingly the most likely of all the relevant historical possibilities. This is the view of the orthodox Marxists of the Leninist persuasion. It is a view, however, that can be held independently of their political program and certainly demands consideration.

The denial that the Russian Revolution was inevitable in the light of Russian social and economic development entails the belief that some other factor was of primary importance. On our hypothesis this factor was the presence of an event-making individual—Lenin. Those who uphold the thesis of inevitability admit that Lenin's presence may have been necessary as far as the *calendar date* of the Russian Revolution was concerned, but, in conformity with their general philosophy of history, affirm that even without him "it would necessarily have come sooner or later." Since our denial of the inevitability of the Russian Revolution is made on the grounds that an event-making personality decided the issue, and that in his absence from the scene events would have fallen out quite differently with profoundly different consequences to the world, the second and third steps of our argument will be considered together.

The contention that the Russian Revolution was historically inevitable rests upon two main lines of evidence. The first consists in the accumulation of data which indicate that, although Russia was predominately a backward agricultural country, she also possessed a highly developed industry with a class conscious proletariat. The standing need of the Russian peasants for land, the dislocations in industry produced by the war, the prevalent mood of war-weariness, and the disorganization of the governmental apparatus produced a revolutionary situation which became progressively more acute from February to the eve of October. A revolutionary situation, however, is not yet a revolution. For that a political party is needed. The second line of evidence is then introduced. This consists in showing that the Bolshevik Party, and the Bolshevik Party alone, had the correct program to meet the needs and demands of the great masses of the Russian people. Taken together, the revolutionary situation and party made the October Revolution the only possible historical solution.

Even if nothing in the above account were disputed, the conclusion is a *non sequitur*. There have been other periods in history which showed us a revolutionary situation and a revolutionary party with a "correct" program from its point of view—and the whole summed up to failure—for example, Germany in 1923. Nor is it true that the Bolshevist Party was the only party with the program which, on this analysis, was called for by the situation. The Bolshevik program was really adapted from the official program of the Social Revolutionary Party during this period.[1]

The great difference was that the program of the Social Revolutionary Party remained a paper resolution, completely disregarded by its representatives in the Provisional Government and Soviets, while the Bolshevik Party carried the program out.

Given the situation in Russia, the October Revolution must be regarded as the work of the Bolshevik Party which capitalized for its own political purposes the hunger of the Russian masses for peace, land, and bread. The main problem then is the relation of Lenin to the Bolshevik Party—to its program, strategy, tactics, and will

[1] See, for documentation, Chernov, *The Great Russian Revolution*, English translation, 1936, Yale University Press, especially Chapter XIX, pp. 392-402. The left wing of this party, it should be recalled here, joined the Bolsheviks in October.

to action. Before we consider it, we should observe that, in fact, the leading role of the Bolshevik Party in the events that culminated in the seizure of power is disputed by none. In question is only the extent to which the Bolshevik Party influenced the restless mood of the Russian masses. Miliukov, typical of the historians of the right, holds their agitation largely responsible for the existence of the mass attitudes which they thereupon skillfully exploited. Trotsky, typical of the historians of the left, maintains that the Bolsheviks from first to last lagged behind the temper of the workers and peasants. Kerensky, speaking for the center, asserts that "the psychology of absolute distrust for the authorities" was aroused in the masses primarily by the attempted *coup d'état* of Kornilov, aided by the friends of Miliukov; the Bolsheviks did the rest.[1] But no matter how the mood of the Russian masses was created, it did not make the Russian Revolution. That was the work of the Bolshevik Party.

But without Nicolai Lenin the work of the Bolshevik Party from April to October 1917 is unthinkable. Anyone who familiarizes himself with its internal history will discover that objectives, policy, slogans, controlling strategy, day-by-day tactics were laid down by Lenin. Sometimes he counseled in the same painstaking way that a tutor coaches a spirited but bewildered pupil; sometimes he commanded like an impatient drill sergeant barking at a raw recruit. But from first to last it was Lenin. Without him there would have been no October Revolution. Here is the evidence.

[1] Kerensky's *Prelude to Bolshevism,* English translation, p. 277, New York, 1919.

a. Until Lenin's return to Russia on April 3, and his presentation of his thesis of April 4, the Bolshevik Party and its official organ were supporting the Provisional Government of Kerensky. Lenin's April Theses, which called for the overthrow of this government by armed insurrection and for all power to the Soviets, came as a bombshell in his own party.

Speaking of the position of the Bolshevik Party in Russia before Lenin arrived, Joseph Stalin wrote on November 19, 1924:

> This position was utterly erroneous, for it begot pacifist illusions, poured water on the mill of defensism and hampered the revolutionary education of the masses. In those days I shared this erroneous position with other Party comrades, and completely renounced it only in the middle of April, when I endorsed Lenin's thesis.[1]

At the beginning Lenin was absolutely alone in his stand. His intransigent demand for immediate cessation of the war against Germany, his call "to turn the imperialist war into a civil war," outraged all political parties. It played into the hands of his enemies who desperately sought to pin on him the false label of "German agent."[2] Nonetheless, before the month was out Lenin

---

[1] Stalin, *The October Revolution*, p. 76. English translation by Cooperative Publishing Society of Foreign Workers in the U.S.S.R., Moscow, 1934. Also issued in New York, 1934.

[2] After all, so the main charge ran, Ludendorff had given him passage through Germany from Switzerland to Russia in the famous sealed train! Where the will to believe is present, and it always is in politics, a great deal can be made of Lenin's act, although it was undertaken before the eyes of the whole world. It would probably have been sufficient evidence to convict Lenin of treason in the Moscow Trials of 1936-1937 had he been alive then.

had converted the executive committee and the most active spirits of his party. Before his arrival the local Bolsheviks were seriously considering organic fusion with the Mensheviks. Lenin changed all that. He drew a sharp line of division between his own party and all the other working-class parties that refused to accept his program.

The significance of Lenin's work in arming his party with a new set of objectives may be gauged by the fact that this involved abandoning doctrines the Bolsheviks had firmly held for an entire decade. Until the February Revolution, all Bolsheviks, including Lenin, believed in what they called "the democratic dictatorship of the workers and peasants." The task of this regime would be to carry out in Russia the achievements of the democratic revolutions of the west. In 1917 Lenin changed his position and that of his party. The Russian Revolution was to be the first breach in the world economy of capitalism. It was to be a "dictatorship of the proletariat" that would stimulate similar dictatorships in the west which co-operatively would initiate the transition to world socialism.

His opponents predicted that Lenin's program would not appease the hunger of the Russian masses for peace, land, and bread; that world-wide socialist revolutions would not follow upon the dictatorship of the proletariat in Europe; that Russia would be devastated by civil war and chaos; that the autocracy of the Czarist bureaucrats and landlords would be replaced by an even more ruthless autocracy of Bolshevik bureaucrats. Despite all criticism from without as well as within his own party, Lenin won his way without yielding an inch.

b. Once Lenin had converted his party to the program of civil war and armed insurrection against the democratic Provisional Government, the main task was clear. It was to choose the proper moment to strike. Until that moment, Lenin was careful to exploit the status of legality in order to carry on his propaganda for overthrow, and to accumulate weapons. After the abrupt turn had been made from critical collaboration to outright opposition, it was not easy to restrain the Bolshevik rank and file, its periphery and sympathizers, from precipitating matters prematurely. If one shoots at a king, one must not miss. And if an insurrection is begun, it is death to fail. Lenin, therefore, was compelled to keep a very close check on the more exuberant of his followers as well as on the mass outbursts that rose periodically as a consequence of delay in meeting the urgent, immediate demands of workers and peasants. He had to forestall an attempt to seize power when the chances were unfavorable for winning it, or holding it after it was won.

During the June days, and much more so during early July, extremist sentiment was rife in influential sections of the Petrograd working class and military garrison. Even some of the Bolshevik leaders were toying with the idea of giving the signal for an all-out attack against the Kerensky government. It was Lenin who held them back. He warned that they would be unable to finish what they started, that they would be crushed, and that the opportunity to strike for power would be lost, perhaps forever. Even so, a considerable number of workers got out of control and appeared on the streets with rifles in their hands. Although they had tried to call off this demonstration, which was largely the result of their previous agitation, the Bolshevik Party at Lenin's command placed itself at its head in order to prevent it from going over into open insurrection. The Bolsheviks were successful in this. But because the Party had taken public responsibility for the armed demonstration, their apparatus was forced underground and they suffered a considerable loss of political influence on the masses. They regained their influence and partially emerged from illegality only after Kornilov attempted his *coup d'état* from the right against the Kerensky government.

c. The most decisive period in Lenin's career of mastery over the Bolshevik Party was the very eve of the October Revolution. Although in hiding, Lenin kept in close touch with the moods of the discontented soldiery and peasants. He was well informed of the disposition of military forces in and about the capital. The Central Committee of the Bolshevik Party, having learned the lesson of the July days, was inclined to go slow. The very furthest thing from their minds was the desire to go over to an open offensive when they received word from Lenin that it was *now or never.*

At first Lenin was in the minority. He raged and stormed. He threatened to go over their heads to the lower party functionaries and to organize matters without them. He wrote letters to influential party members to get them to bring pressure on the lagging executive committee. After fierce and stubborn debate, he won them to his position. How urgent Lenin considered the period they were in—as *the* period in which to stake all on a bid for power—is apparent from his letter of October 21, 1917, to the Central Executive Committee, demanding the organization of an armed insurrection during the next few days: "The success of both the Russian and world revolution depends upon two or three days of struggle." [1] When he finally won his majority by a vote of ten to two, the die was cast. The Bolsheviks took state power.

d. That they kept state power during the subsequent year was again due primarily to Lenin's guiding policy. One group of the Central Committee desired to continue the war against Hohenzollern Germany while appealing to the German workers to emulate the Bolsheviks. Another group advocated the policy of "neither peace nor war." Lenin stood firm for a signed treaty of peace which would give the Bolsheviks respite from their foreign enemy for the moment and sufficient time to consolidate themselves against their internal foes. During these days, Lenin was again a hopeless minority at first but hammered away until his colleagues yielded. The Treaty of Brest-Litovsk was signed.

If Lenin had not returned to Russia or had died en route, there is no evidence whatsoever to support the hypothesis that Kamenev, Muranov, and Stalin, then in control of Bolshevik policy, would have reversed helm and taken up war to the end against the democratic provisional Government. If during June and July Lenin had

[1] *Collected Works*, English translation, vol. 21, p. 99, New York, 1932.

not been present to prevail upon the excited spirits among the Bolsheviks and other *Enragés* and forestall an uprising, the whole organization would have been destroyed in blood. If, on the eve of October, the Bolsheviks had marked time despite Lenin's exhortations, Kerensky would have been able to garrison the capitol with reliable troops and easily cope with the Bolsheviks. If Lenin had not stopped the Germans by giving them all they wanted, their army would have taken both Petrograd and Moscow, since military resistance was no longer possible. Lenin and his colleagues would either have met the fate of Karl Liebknecht and Rosa Luxemburg in Germany or would have been dispersed to the four corners of the vast Russian land.

Lenin, of course, was not the Bolshevik Party. But the Bolshevik Party became the instrument it did because of Lenin. It is doubtful whether any man before him ever wielded such power in a political party; certainly not in an organization that professed to be democratic or socialistic.

If Lenin had not been on the scene, not a single revolutionary leader could have substituted for him. Not Stalin, by his own confession. Not Zinoviev, Lenin's closest follower, who ran out on the October Revolution. Not Kamenev, whose mind Lenin changed at the same time he changed Stalin's, but who acted like Zinoviev. Not Trotsky. Although the record shows that Trotsky was the only outstanding Russian figure whose theoretical position and practical program were identical with those of Lenin *before* April 1917, he would have failed where Lenin succeeded. For one thing, he arrived in Russia a month after Lenin did. By that time Lenin had completed the reeducation of the Bolshevik Party. Trotsky would have had to do this, but he was not a member of the organization. His own party was numerically insignificant and relatively uninfluential. Finally, he owed whatever authority he enjoyed in the Bolshevik Party, which he joined in August, to Lenin's recognition of his capacities and Lenin's constant protection against the suspicion and opposition of the second-line Bolshevik leaders. Trotsky, alone, was doomed to failure because, despite his other great gifts, he lacked the organizational genius so necessary for political success. His imperious manner provoked people instead of reconciling them to his capacities. He could win an audience but, unlike Lenin, he could not win over party opponents. And he openly betrayed an impatience with mediocrity which no one forgives in a newcomer.

4

What would have been the consequences for history if the October Revolution had not occurred or, occuring, had failed? It is easier to say what would *not* have happened than to say with any great degree of definiteness what *would* have happened. Here the possibility is always present that events from other series of happenings might erupt into the series we are considering, like comets that crash into a solar system and upset its otherwise calculable behavior. But we are entitled to make a rough chart of what might have been on the basis of what we already know. If this is disputed in principle, as we have seen, the possibility of all grounded prediction in human and historical affairs must be ruled out.

If the Bolsheviks had lost their golden hour, the left Social Revolutionaries together with some anarchist groups might have attempted to seize power. But it is extremely unlikely that they could have achieved more than a noisy disturbance. They had no organizational discipline and could hardly formulate, much less execute, a centralized plan of control. Even in the unlikely event of victory, their program would have stopped where that of the Bolsheviks began—with the land in the hands of the peasants.

The Russian military front would have collapsed anyhow. The truth was that, by the end of 1917, there was no military front. The Germans could have advanced at will at any time. An armistice with Germany was unavoidable no matter who constituted the government. The Constituent Assembly, Russia's parliamentary democracy, which was bayoneted out of existence at its first session by the Bolsheviks, would in all likelihood have converted Russia into a constitutional republic on the model of France and England. The preponderance of Socialist sentiment guaranteed a highly advanced system of social legislation. The banks and some of the basic public services and industries would probably have been socialized, but there would have been no collectivization of industry. The Russian market would have been opened as a vast field for European industry. The catastrophic world crisis which began in 1928 would have probably been delayed, and in any event its effects appreciably mitigated when it did occur. Fascist parties would have existed as political sects, but Fascism as a mass movement would not have developed in the face of a united European working class.

Even without the October Revolution, the *danger* of war would not have been removed. For conflicts between national economies for the exploitation of the world market would still have continued in the absence of some form of planned economy to undergird a world political union. In the east, developments would have been pretty much the same as they were, particularly as far as Japan is concerned. But in the west, in the absence of Fascism, war might have been avoided although its danger would not have been dispelled. A democratic Russia in the League of Nations from the very beginning would have been a natural ally of the Weimar Republic, and the worst features of the Versailles system would have been obviated. A reconstituted socialist and labor international might perhaps have emerged from the carnage of the first war, mindful of the opportunities it missed in 1914 and powerful enough to prevent the settling of economic issues by the trial of arms.

Some historians admit that the victory of the October Revolution was not determined, in the sense that it was the sole historical possibility in the situation. But they maintain that if there had not been an October, or if it had failed, the only other alternative was the restoration of Czarism: "The alternative to Tsarism was not constitutional monarchy or liberal republicanism, but Bolshevism. . . . The alternative to Bolshevism, had it failed to survive the ordeal of civil war . . . would not have been Chernov, elected according to the most modern rules of equal suffrage and proportional representation, but a military dictator, a Kolchak or a Denikin. . . ." [1] This is a very widely entertained view, but we believe it to be mistaken.

The counterrevolutionary movement of Kornilov before October dissolved like snow in a hot sun. What made it possible for Kolchak and Denikin to resume? Foreign support—a foreign support that would have been completely absent if a democratic regime had continued to exist in Russia. The Bolshevik dictatorship was in fact strengthened by foreign intervention. Many who were hostile to the Bolsheviks' political rule fought side by side with them because they regarded the civil war as a national war against invaders. The Czarists in fact had very little social support in Russia, and what they had was drawn from the large landlords and their dependents. The peasants kept their fists on the land. When they had a choice, they preferred the Bolsheviks, who *promised* to let them keep it, to the counterrevolutionists who took the land away from them. There would probably have been no new insurrection from the right if the Constituent Assembly had been permitted to enjoy its legitimate authority. And in the improbable event that

[1] William Henry Chamberlin, *The Russian Revolution,* vol. I, p. 371, New York, 1935. In many respects this book is the most objective account of the period so far written.

it would have occurred, it would have been very brief, for it would have faced a practically unified people.

The reasons usually advanced for the impossibility of Russia's finding a democratic mean between the autocracy of Czarism and the autocracy of Bolshevism are such that they would also "prove" the English and French Revolutions impossible.

Our main concern, however, is not with the particular historical picture that would have unrolled itself if there had been no October. And at this point we are not at all concerned with its desirability. We believe that whether the world would have been happier or unhappier, better or worse, at any rate it would have been tremendously different; that future historians will consider the October Revolution as a turning point which opened a new era of weal and woe in the history of mankind; and that, on the available evidence, they will attribute to the event-making character of Nicolai Lenin the chief role in the achievement of that revolution.

*　　*　　*　　*

The foregoing analysis of the event-making significance of Lenin in the Russian Revolution is still incomplete. It does not warrant acceptance unless it can be sustained against the thesis of one of the outstanding participants in its crucial struggles who maintains that the Russian Revolution was inevitable. In his remarkable *History of the Russian Revolution*, Leon Trotsky undertakes to prove, in conformity with Marxist principles, that the October Revolution was the only path possible

in the development of Russia after the downfall of Czarism. His work abounds with sentences like: "The October Revolution advanced with a physical necessity." It
has "a deep natural inevitability." It exemplifies "that
mighty development of great revolutions." [1] Despite its
obvious bias, which the author makes no effort to con-
ceal, his study is a historical document of the first importance for an understanding of the period from February
to October 1917. It is the most plausible account the
Bolsheviks have given of themselves.

But does it confirm his thesis?

In all of his historical writing two souls struggle within
Trotsky's breast—the soul of the orthodox Marxist who
must interpret history in line with the dogmas of his
monistic creed, and the soul of the empirical investigator
who must follow the evidence where it leads. Events can
never refute the creed of historical materialsm: it is
necessary only to interpret them properly. The scientific
historian, however, must bow before the stubborn fact.
We shall show that what his creedal soul proposes is at
odds with what his empirical investigation discloses.

Trotsky's empirical analysis does establish on the basis
of incontestable evidence, the powerlessness of the Czarist system to survive any large-scale war. Even without
a war, it was rotten, ripe for collapse. It would probably
have gone under in the next wave of internal disturbance.
And by the end of the first year of war, even the nobility
was already drawing lots to determine who was to kill
Nicholas II and his entourage. But there is still a long

---

[1] *Op. cit.*, vol. I, p. 460, vol. III, p. 260.

way to go from the doom of Czarism to the inevitability (or overwhelming probability) of the October Revolution. Trotsky attempts to bridge this gap by showing that Russia in 1917, under any regime, was unable to continue fighting and that, without the solution of the land problem, the country, whether at peace or war, could not escape chaos. Here, too, the contentions are amply supported by evidence. Yet it still does not follow from them that the triumph of the Bolshevik Party was historically necessary.

After all, we have already seen that an early peace and the division of the landed estates were a part of the program of the Social Revolutionary Party. Had the October Revolution failed, the physical inability to continue the war, as well as the necessity of safeguarding the country from possible new uprisings by the followers of Kornilov on the one hand and Lenin on the other, would have compelled the Constituent Assembly to come to terms with Germany. And as for satisfying the peasantry, there was no *arrière pensée* behind the concern of the Social Revolutionary Party with giving land to the peasants, as there was with the Bolsheviks. Despite its heterogeneous social composition, the Social Revolutionary Party was primarily a peasant party. It refused to countenance seizure of land out of hand because of its desire to regularize division of the estates. It waited for the Constituent Assembly to do this. But the peasants were tired of waiting for land, the soldiers were tired of waiting for peace, and the workers were tired of food shortages and rising prices.

Without challenging a single one of his facts (and some are not above challenge), one may say that all Trotsky has proved is that the objective historical situation made a Bolshevik triumph possible. But the question is: what transformed the possibility into an actuality? Could that possibility have been lost? Why in fact was it not lost?

His answer rises out of every crucial page where he is discussing events and not defending a faith. It was not lost because of the leadership of Lenin. But this answer gives Lenin such stature as an event-making figure in history that it flouts a cherished dogma of Trotsky's Marxism. In consequence, when Trotsky is compelled by his own narrative to face the question squarely, his reply takes the form of a series of stammering evasions. A "yes" alternates with a "no" in a kind of double talk that defies even the mystical logic of dialectic and peters out lamely in a change of subject. The general upshot of the key passage is a cautious admission that without Lenin the October Revolution might not have occurred. But this is immediately counteracted by subsequent passages in which Trotsky denies the legitimacy of the very question he has asked and tried to answer.

It remains to ask—and this is no unimportant question, although easier to ask than to answer: How would the revolution have developed if Lenin had not reached Russia in April 1917? If our exposition demonstrates and proves anything at all, we hope it proves that Lenin was not a demiurge of the revolutionary process, that he merely (!) entered into a chain of objective historical forces. But he was a great link in that chain. The dictatorship of the proletariat was to be inferred from the whole situation, but it still had to be established. It could not be established without a party. The party could fulfill its mission only after understanding it. For that Lenin was needed. Until his arrival, not one of the Bolshevik leaders dared to make a diagnosis of the revolution. . . . Inner struggle in the Bolshevik Party was absolutely unavoidable. Lenin's arrival merely (!) hastened the process. His personal influence shortened the crisis. Is it possible, however, to say confidently that the party without him would have found its road? We would by no means make bold to say that. The factor of time is decisive here and it is difficult in retrospect to tell time historically. Dialectic materialism at any rate has nothing in common with fatalism.[1]

If one were to ferret out a meaning from the twists and turns of this passage, it would seem to support the conclusion we have previously reached. But that impression is immediately canceled by Trotsky's refusal to dissociate Lenin from the situation in which he found himself. He tells us that it is mechanical and one-sided to juxtapose Lenin, on the one hand, "the person, the hero, the genius," and the objective conditions on the other, "the mass, the party." In order to keep his doctrinal piety unflecked by the stain of heresy, Trotsky unknowingly reverts to the position of Herbert Spencer. Spencer dismissed the question of the relation between the outstanding individual and his time on the ground that a man and his period had to be considered together

[1] *Op. cit.* vol. I, pp. 329-330. See also vol. III, p. 154.

and that *both* were determined by the antecedent state of culture.

Trotsky, too, disallows any comparison between Lenin and the conditions of his time, including the masses and party, because they are all explained by something else. He assures us that Lenin was not an accidental element in the historical development of Russia and that *both* Lenin and his party were "a product of the whole past of Russian history." Naturally! Of what else could they be a historical product? But what bearing has this tautology on the question: would the Bolshevik Party have found its way to October without Lenin? No matter what historical events had happened from February to October, we would still be able to say, with as much reason as Trotsky, that it was a product of the whole past of Russian history. Since such a phrase could "explain" both the success of the Bolsheviks with Lenin and their failure without him, it is completely irrelevant to the question. To relapse into outright mysticism, all Trotsky need do is to assert that the existence of a Lenin in Russia in 1917 was assured by the whole past of Russian history. Providence sends us the Man of God, and the Mephistophelean dialectic, *der Geist der stets verneint*, sends us the Man of the People.

The phrase "product of the whole past of Russian history" can be given a definite meaning. In this sense, anything is a "product" of past Russian history if, *before* its occurrence, it can be, or could have been predicted on the available historical evidence as the only likely alternative of future development. In this use of the phrase we are justified in concluding that the best evidence, including the evidence presented by Trotsky, shows that the Russian Revolution of October 1917 was *not* so much a product of the whole past of Russian history as a product of one of the most event-making figures of all time.

*   *   *   *

What manner of man was Lenin who filled this event-making role in history? Under the circumstances, our curiosity is entirely legitimate, because it is the *character* of the individual which chiefly distinguishes the eventful man from the event-making man. What we are particularly interested in is discovering the combination of characteristics which gave Lenin political pre-eminence over a galaxy of individuals who as thinkers, writers, and mass orators displayed greater talents than he possessed. Analysis of this, as of any form of genius, is difficult to make. Particularly in politics, a medium in which virtues and vices, reason and stupidity, have an entirely different specific gravity than in the clear waters of personal relations and scientific activity, is it difficult to evaluate genius. No bare enumeration of character traits can do justice to the power of insight which flashes to the surface when these traits operate together in the context of problems, dangers, ideal goals.

One of the most conspicuous expressions of political insight is the sense of timing. Without it, great intelligence can be ineffective. Coupled with strong will, it can carry a mediocre mind to the heights. No one who knew, say, Plechanov and Stalin before February expected that one would fade out of the historical picture so soon and that the other would gradually emerge as the strong man of the strongest party. But it was Lenin's superb sense of political timing, nourished by an intelligence more practical than Plechanov's and a will more inflexible than Stalin's, that won an empire for the Bolsheviks.

Every adequate analysis of Lenin, the political man, must note his stubborn tenacity of purpose and unsurpassable confidence in himself. If he ever harbored a doubt about the ultimate success of his cause, the rightness of his tactical decisions, the high price of victory paid out in human suffering and injustice, he never expressed it to anyone. He was beyond the corruptions of pleasure and immune to the impractical delights of thought. His basic allegiance was to certain simple ideal socialist goals which were at the same time so vague that, given the consciousness of his own absolute integrity, he could always justify to himself what *he* did despite appearances.

Lenin could influence human beings only within the framework of organization. He had no power as an individual with the masses. Although unpretentious, he lacked the common touch which wins the masses by a radiant sympathy; and although he always had something to tell them, he could not strike the sparks of fire to inflame them into action.

Lenin was a party man. The life of the party was spiritual meat and substance to him. Just as some men's personalities are sustained by a church, and others are enriched by the passions and crises and problems of love, family, and knowledge, so Lenin's personality was sustained by, and developed within, the party. He was never far from the center of any organization of which he was a member. In his own mind, wherever he was, *there* was the party. His passions, his problems, his judgments all reflect this intense concentration on the party —a concentration which was all the more selfless because subconsciously he was the party. Whether he considered problems of state or art or philosophy, there was not a disinterested nerve in his body. In fact, all problems were for him problems of politics, even the listening to music and the playing of chess.

Lenin was not merely a party man. He raised the party to the level of a political principle. This is the source of all his deviations from the essentially democratic views of Marx. For Marx, a political party was conceived as a kind of cross between an international educational institution for the working class and a pressure group, as something that would come and go and be reconstituted in the forge of historical events. But for Lenin the political party was an army of professional revolutionists. The organization of professional revolutionists was of supreme importance in capturing state power. Iron-clad control of organization was essential to victory. This ideal organization must, like Lenin himself, be acutely sensitive to the moods of the masses. It must have a perfect sense of timing. And above all, it must be imbued with the unshakeable conviction that it knew what the true interests of the masses were, better than they did themselves. In the light of this knowledge, it was justified in promising them anything to get them to move, and in manipulating them into actions which, even if they were foredoomed to failure, would educate them up to a level of Bolshevik understanding. The professional revolutionist by definition was one who wanted nothing for himself, and in fact cared so little for material goods that he could sincerely believe that he was free from the temptations and corruptions of absolute power.

Lenin was a Marxist who interchanged the "dictatorship of the proletariat"—which for Marx was a *broader* democracy of the working class counterposed to the narrower democracy of capitalist society—with the outright dictatorship of a minority Communist Party *over* the proletariat. Lenin believed that the hope of mankind lay in the struggle of the working class to abolish capitalism and therewith all economic classes. But he was even more convinced that this struggle could be successful *only* when led by his own party no matter what its name. He did not flinch from the inexorable conclusion that, therefore, any individual or group who opposed *the* Party was objectively "an enemy of mankind."

At one stroke all other parties of the working class were thrust on the other side of the barricades. Lenin not only used the method of "amalgam" against them, he believed it. The method of amalgam was to link up a Kronstadt sailor fighting for Soviet democracy against party dictatorship with the Black Hundreds of Czarism, to identify a socialist critic of Bolshevism, who had languished for years in prerevolutionary prisons, with partisans of Denikin and Kolchak. Before Lenin died, *anyone* who called for Soviet democracy as opposed to party dictatorship was forthwith denounced as a counterrevolutionist. This seems ironical because Lenin's chief slogan against Kerensky had been "All Power to the Soviets." But Lenin would have failed to see any irony whatever in such a situation. Slogans, like people, had to be used in a functional or, to use his own expression, in a "concrete" way, that is, to carry forward the political task of the moment. The goal in behalf of which political tasks were to be solved was power for the Bolsheviks. Thus, when it seemed necessary for the victory of the party, Lenin proclaimed "All Power to the Soviets." In July, when it seemed that the Bolsheviks could not capture the Soviets, Lenin denounced the slogan and looked around for other agencies through which power could be won. Later, when the situation once more made the prospect of Bolshevik capture of the Soviets favorable, Lenin returned to the old slogan. But after power was won in October, Soviet democracy meant the possibility that the Bolsheviks might lose power. To Lenin this was plain counterrevolution.

Had he been consistent, Lenin would have also drawn the conclusion that anyone *within* his party who opposed his policies was also objectively an enemy of mankind. But he showed his genius by following not the logic of his position but the needs of successful organization. He displayed great aptitude in using and winning for his purposes those in his own ranks who disagreed with him. He could work with people who without him could not work with each other. It was left to Stalin to draw the logical conclusion, and to convict any opponent on any matter of being an enemy of humanity. But that was when Lenin's party did not have to make a revolution.

In contrast to the entire field of his rivals in the period from February to October, Lenin knew what he wanted —power. In contrast to them, he knew how important a political army was and how it could best be deployed to achieve power. And in contrast to them once more, he dared all on his program and on himself. Like the good dialectical materialist he was, his faith was nothing short of cosmic. Compared to Lenin with his deep belief in himself as an instrument of historic necessity, Cromwell, who inwardly trembled lest his soul be lost, appears like an introspective character out of a prerevolutionary Russian novel.

Karl Kautsky once characterized Lenin as the Russian Bismarck. In calling attention to the masterly game of revolutionary *Real-Politik* Lenin played, the comparison is apt. But Junker that he was, Bismark was a divided character. He had no more religion than Napoleon and fancied himself as a kind of Norse hero wresting an empire from the designs of a malignant Fate. Lenin was all of a piece. He created an empire as if it were on order and pretended sincerely that he was merely following out a recipe laid down by Marx and Engels, his holy authorities. A story circulated among the Bolsheviks after his death would have pleased his pious heart. Lenin appeared before the Gates of St. Peter and knocked for admission. "Who are you?" asked St. Peter. To which, instead of giving his name, Lenin modestly replied: "I am the interest on Marx's *Capital*." [1]

The sense of his historic mission freed Lenin from any shame, embarrassment, and regret in revising his course or in zigzagging from one position to another. He accepted *practical* responsibility, but in his own mind history absolved him from all *moral* responsibility. What would have been utter hypocrisy in a man of little faith appeared in him as flexible intelligence wrestling with the exigencies attendant upon implementing high principle. It is characteristic that those who struggled with him most bitterly in the arena of revolutionary struggle—where no blows or holds are barred—acknowledge his absolute sincerity and his moral force on others. They were fascinated by him even when they most detested him. He wanted nothing for himself—except to determine the destiny of mankind. His judgment could not be swayed by women, friends, or comforts, or tempered by mercy or pity. When Berkman and Goldman pleaded with him to release imprisoned anarchists who had criticized the Bolsheviks, he replied in effect: "Genuine, thinking anarchists, agree with us: only bandits posing as anarchists are in jail." [2] This was monstrously false—but undoubtedly Lenin believed it. When he advised foreign Communists, introducing Trojan horses into democratic organizations, to lie about their beliefs and membership, he was firmly convinced that this would be

---

[1] I give for whatever it is worth an emendation of this story that circulated among the democratic socialists of the west. To St. Peter's question, Lenin replies: "I am the interest on Marx's *Capital*. Marx is below and has slammed the gates of Hell in my face."

[2] Emma Goldman, *Living My Life*, p. 764, New York, 1931.

loyalty to a "higher" truth. When Otto Bauer interpreted the New Economic Policy introduced by Lenin as a partial return to capitalism, Lenin complained, and with honest indignation: "And the Mensheviks and Social-Revolutionaries, all of whom preach this sort of thing, are astonished when we say that we will shoot those who say such things." [1] What is significant here, as elsewhere, is the way Lenin takes it for granted that the rights of opposition he claimed for himself when he was *out* of power are completely without validity when claimed by others when he is *in* power.

Few pen portraits or biographies of Lenin of any worth have until now been written. What we have are primarily contributions to the fierce factional disputes that raged after Lenin's death. It is to the relatively scant characterizations of Lenin written while he was still alive that we must go for a reliable account of the way he impressed the men who worked with him. That is why the following lines by A. V. Lunacharsky, a keen observer and coworker of Lenin, are so telling. "Lenin does his work imperiously, not because power is sweet to him, but because he is sure he is right, and cannot endure to have anybody spoil his work. His love of power grows out of his tremendous sureness and the correctness of his principles, and if you please, out of an inability (very useful in a political leader) to see from the point of view of his opponents." [2]

---

[1] *Selected Works*, vol. IX, p. 342.
[2] *Revolutionary Silhouettes*, Moscow, 1923, quoted by Max Eastman in his introduction to the English translation of Trotsky's *History of the Russian Revolution*, vol. I., p. xv.

Pit a man of this "tremendous sureness," imperious will and drive, organizational genius, and sensitiveness to the psychology of the crowd against the golden opportunity of national demoralization following an exhausting war—and the issue of who will rule whom will never remain long in doubt.

*　　*　　*　　*

Henri Poincaré, a great French physicist, discussing chance and history, tells us that: "The greatest bit of chance is the birth of a great man." This is true in a twofold sense. The biological potentialities of the hero cannot be derived from the laws of social behavior. Nor can they be derived from the laws of heredity, since the latter are general and statistical in form while it is this particular conjunction of germinal cells that gives us the individual hero. But once the potentially great man is born, and so long as he remains on the scene, his influence on affairs is not a matter of chance. Under certain circumstances this influence may be broadly calculable although not necessary just as we may be able to anticipate the effects of foolishness or wisdom in military, industrial, and political leadership. Once the hero is on the scene, to what extent should we and can we control him? This question is particularly pertinent for the intelligent democrat.

XI *The Hero and Democracy*

Iғ ᴛʜᴇ ʜᴇʀᴏ is defined as an event-making individual who redetermines the course of history, it follows at once that a democratic community must be eternally on guard against him.

This simple, and to some unwelcome, conclusion is involved in the very conception of a democratic society. For in such a society leadership cannot arrogate to itself heroic power. At legally determined intervals government must draw its sanction from the *freely given consent* of the governed. And so long as that consent is *freely* given, that is, after the opposition has been heard, the policy or action agreed upon becomes the one for which the community is responsible even though the leadership may have initiated it.[1]

The problem of leadership in a democracy is highly

[1] For further amplification of the meaning of "freely given consent," see Chapter thirteen of my *Reason, Social Myths and Democracy*, New York, 1941; also "The Philosophical Presuppositions of Democracy," *Ethics*, April 1942.

complex. Its importance warrants further clarification. Our reflections in this chapter, as distinct from the others, will be normative. They will involve judgments of value concerning democracy and democracy's good.

An old Chinese proverb tells us "the great man is a public misfortune." The sentiment aptly expresses the experience and wisdom of a peace-loving race. Were the victims of great men's glory to speak, not only in China but almost anywhere, they would echo this homely judgment with sighs and tears and curses. For on the whole, heroes in history have carved out their paths of greatness by wars, conquests, revolutions, and holy crusades.

And yet this Chinese proverb epitomizes only past history, and not all of that. A great man may sometimes be a public fortune. His absence is far from being a sign that we shall be spared great misfortunes. Indeed, in face of calamity the people pray for a deliverer. Among the calamities they pray to be delivered from may be the rule of an earlier deliverer. If we were to conclude from the evil things great men have done that their greatness is the source of their evil, we should have to condemn all talent and capacity because they are often abused.

Great men, then, may be good men. And still a democracy must be suspicious of them! For essential to democracy is the participation of the governed in determining their own welfare. This participation is coupled with the *hope* that the governed will select and elect their governors wisely, that is, in such a way as to gratify as many of their needs and wants as the situation permits. But more important than this hope, which is sometimes sadly at variance with the facts, is the belief that it is more worthy of men to decide their own fate than to let others decide it for them.

The hero in a democratic community—the potentially event-making man—may sincerely believe that he accepts its underlying philosophy. But sooner or later he finds himself straining against two features of the democratic process. The first is the principle of majority rule, especially when he is convinced that the majority is wrong on a matter of great import. The second is the slowness of its operation even when he believes the majority is right.

No one believes in majority rule as a reasonable principle of decision in a family of small children, a prison, or an institution for the feeble-minded. To the extent that we accept majority rule as an essential feature of democracy, we are committed to the well-grounded belief that, on the whole, men are not infants, cretins, or criminals. But although men are capable of rationality, reason in human affairs is so much a matter of weighing interests, and interests so often are at variance with each other, that the majority's reason may be the minority's disaster. This proves that the principle of majority rule is not sufficient for democracy, not that it is unnecessary. Nor does it prove that certain rights are inalienable and absolute, for not one such right can be mentioned which under certain circumstances may not need to be abridged in the interest of other rights.

What is necessary in addition to the principle of majority rule is the recognition by every group interest in society of the legitimacy of any group interest, provided the group in question accepts the methods of *free* in-inquiry and democratic decision as principles of negotiating conflicts of interest. Even so the majority may be mistaken and unjust, even as the man who follows the lead of evidence may sometimes be mistaken while the man who acts blindly may be right. But the majority that provides a minority with the possibility of becoming a majority through the education of citizens by public opposition has gone as far as it can politically to meet legitimate grievance. Under the conditions indicated, the democrat who enjoys freedom of agitation must abide by the decision of the majority even when he believes it to be wrong.

This does not *in principle* justify toleration of a minority whose actual program calls for the overthrow of democratic political institutions by force of arms. Any particular minority may be tolerated on grounds of prudence or expediency, for example, where it is opposed to another minority, more dangerous at the moment, or where its suppression is likely to establish a precedent that may be extended to other minorities who are genuinely devoted to democratic processes.

*   *   *   *

The "potential hero" in a democracy sees what others do not. His will to action is stronger. His knowledge of what must be done to realize what he sees is surer. For these reasons, he finds himself, more likely than not, in a minority. His sense of his vocation impels him to fight for his insight. His loyalty to the democratic ideal compels him to make this insight the common faith of the majority. If the latter remain stubbornly intractable, his chances of heroic action, as a democrat, are lost. The hero fades into history as a "village Hamden."

Superior talent and strong vision, however, press for expression. So far as the hero does not renounce politics as a sphere of activity, his task becomes to get himself accepted by a majority. For, as a democrat, he does not dare to admit to himself or to others that he wants to make himself independent of the majority. In pursuit of a majority, he may seek to win it, broadly speaking, by the patient methods of education, relying upon the inherent reasonableness of his vision to make its way.

Insofar as he does this, and only so far, democracy is safe from the hero. This means that he courts failure. But the hero may master the arts of the demagogue and use the very instruments of democracy to debase its quality. Yet as long as democratic controls are not abolished, the hero as demagogue must still build up, cajole, and cater to the majority. He acquires a contempt for the group he leads by virtue of the methods by which he corrupts them. In the process, if his own will and insight grow uncertain and cloudy, he becomes just another politician. He is a hero who has missed his chance. But where his will and insight remain firm, the hero as demagogue must "fool" his following into accepting them. He must develop a public platform, on the basis of which he solicits confidence, and a secret program in whose behalf he uses the confidence so won. He becomes a threat to democracy. The greater his faith in himself, the more disinterested his intentions, the more fateful the issue to which his heroic vision drives him, the more insidious is the menace to the whole rationale of democracy. Particularly so if the hero or potential event-making character believes himself to be the indispensable instrument of his vision.

Until now we have assumed that the standpoint of the hero is one that cannot recommend itself to the majority in the light of free discussion and intelligent inquiry and that if it is adopted it is only in virtue of chicanery and demagogic fraud. Let us now assume that the majority is properly persuaded that the hero is right. The latter may still regard the processes of democracy as a fetter upon his calling. For these processes grind too slowly, and many things will not wait. If he is confident that he knows the community's good, and convinced that it hangs in the balance, the hero is tempted to confront it with a *fait accompli.* Well-intentioned opposition that delays and obstructs appears to him as objective betrayal, and can easily be pilloried as such. And he knows that, if he succeeds, a great deal will be forgiven him.

But need a democracy move slowly? No, for its pace can be accelerated by delegation of power to the leader or hero. Yet in the best of situations, this only mitigates the dangers of delay; it does not eliminate them. For a democracy cannot in advance delegate all its powers and remain a democracy. And the crucial situation is always one that involves the undelegated powers. Since power cannot in a democracy be delegated in perpetuity, the crucial situation may arise just when the delegation of power is up for *renewal*. Again, the delegation of power is always requested in a moment of crisis or emergency. But who is to determine when the moment is here?

The hero always presses for greater powers. It is natural to his vocation that he should do so. He is as eager to accept new powers as he is reluctant to surrender them after they are granted. And it is true that, in a troubled world, no democratic community can survive for long unless it entrusts its leaders with great powers. At the same time, what it gives with reluctance, it must take back with eagerness. The timing is all—and it is not likely that the hero and the community will agree on what time it is.

There cannot be any guarantee that a leader will not usurp delegated power to carry out a heroic event-making task. But a democracy would be foolish to refuse delegation of power for this reason if the situation is so crucial that decisive action must be taken at once. On the other hand, there may be no evidence that delegated powers will be abused. Nonetheless, a democracy would be foolish not to withdraw them promptly when the emergency is over, for they are a standing temptation to abuse and usurpation.

A democracy is imperiled not alone by its heroes, necessary as they may sometimes be for survival. It is imperiled by any group of its citizens who are more attached to the advantages or privileges they enjoy under democracy, or hope it will bring, than they are to the democratic process of bringing them about. For these groups, which set greater store on peace or prosperity or social status than they do on the methods of democracy to preserve (or modify) them, are the ones which feel justified in calling in the hero to cherish their "goods" even at the cost of democracy. An instructive example is furnished by conservative classes in western Europe who, convinced that democratic legislation had unjustly abridged the privileges of property, opened the gates to Mussolini and Hitler. True, their profession of democratic allegiance was merely lip service to begin with. But not so for the large numbers of the middle classes and even workers who constituted the mass base of Fascism. Security, fixed prices, employment meant more to them than democracy. They were to learn that when democracy goes, the goods for which it is sacrificed, without becoming more certain, are degraded in quality.

*　　*　　*　　*

If we were to list as heroes the event-making men of the past, we should find few of them in the histories of democratic societies. It is in conformity with the genius of democratic society that this should be so.

There is great wisdom in the notorious political ingratitude of democratic communities. They usually refuse to glorify their leaders until they are dead. And the best reason for honoring these leaders is that they did not yield to the temptations of power, or that they were prepared to step down from positions of power even when they were convinced that they were right and the majority wrong.

Great men do not ask permission to be born. Nor do they ask permission of democracies to lead them. They find their own way to the tasks they feel called to fulfill, unless crushed by a hostile environment or isolated by the tide of events. Democracies do not have to seek these heroes when it seeks leaders. For if they exist, they will make themselves heard. A democracy must always be girded to protect itself against them even as it uses them, relying not on *their* intentions, which are always honorable but not infrequently messianic, but on the mechanisms of its own democratic institutions, on the plurality of centers of power and interest, and on the spirit of its education and morale.

In a democratic community education must pitch the ideal of the hero in a different key from that of the event-making man. The heroes in a democracy should be the great figures in the Pantheon of thought, the men of ideas, of social vision, of scientific achievement and artistic power. For it is these men who mould the intellectual ideals and social attitudes of the citizens, who without knowledge, quickened perception, and educated taste cannot realize the promise of democracy. If we are earnest in our belief in democracy, we must recognize that it is those who are affected by a basic policy who must pass upon it, either directly or indirectly. And if they are to pass upon it intelligently, know when to delegate power or withdraw it, and enhance the quality of political life by their participation, they must develop a sensitiveness to what is significant and what is trivial, an indifference to rhetorical bombast but a keen interest in what it conceals, an ability to isolate relevant issues and to weigh the available evidence.

The statesman in a democracy exercises his leadership by *proposing* a policy. But whether it is adopted and why depends upon the representatives of the democratic community who are chosen by individuals themselves potentially representatives. A successful democracy, therefore, may honor its statesmen; but it must honor its teachers more—whether they be prophets, scientists, poets, jurists, or philosophers. The true hero of democracy, then, should be not the soldier or the political leader, great as their services may be, but the teacher— the Jeffersons, Holmeses, Deweys, Whitmans, and all others who have given the people vision, method, and knowledge.

It is the task of a democratic society to break down the invidious distinctions reflected in current linguistic usage between the hero and the masses or the average man. This can be accomplished in part by reinterpreting the meaning of the word "hero," and by recognizing that "heroes" can be made by fitting social opportunities more skillfully to specific talents. What we call "the average man" is not a biological but a social phenomenon. Human capacities are much more diversified than our social arrangements take note of.

Where we restrict social opportunities, so that only a few types of excellence are recognized, in respect to them the great mass of individuals, despite their differences, will appear as the dull, gray average. If, however, we extend social opportunities so that each per-

son's specific talents have a stimulus to development and
expression, we increase the range of possibility of dis-
tinctively significant work. From this point of view, a
hero is any individual who does his work well and makes
a unique contribution to the public good. It is sheer prej-
udice to believe that the grandeur and nobility associated with the heroic life can be found only in careers
that reck little of human blood and suffering. Daily toil
on any level has its own occasions of struggle, victory,
and quiet death. A democracy should contrive its affairs,
not to give one or a few the chance to reach heroic
stature, but rather to take as a regulative ideal the slogan,
"every man a hero."

We call this a "regulative ideal" because it would be
Utopian to imagine that it could ever be literally embodied. As a regulative ideal it gives direction to policies
that enable society to make the best of whatever powers
are available to men.

What are the powers available to men? They are theoretically limited but practically indefinite. In the absence
of an environment that encourages their expression, no
one can speak with dogmatism about their nature and
specific form. Nor can we be certain of the precise limit
of human power without allowing for the willed effort
that enables the runner to clear a hurdle that until then
had been an insuperable obstacle.

A democracy should encourage the belief that all are
called and all may be chosen. All may be chosen because
a wisely contrived society will take as a point of departure the rich possibilities that nature herself gives through

the spontaneous variations in the powers and capacities of men. These variations are the source and promise of new shoots of personality and value. The belief that all may be chosen, acted upon in a co-operating environment, may inspire the added increment of effort that often transforms promise into achievement.

*　　*　　*　　*

Our conception of a democracy without event-making figures runs counter to a plausible but fundamentally mistaken critique of democracy developed by a notable school of Italian theorists—Mosca, Pareto, and Michels.[1] These men in different ways seek to establish the impossibility of democracy. Their chief argument is that all political rule involves organization and that all organization, no matter how democratic its mythology, sooner or later comes under the effective control of a minority élite. The history of societies, despite the succession of different political *forms*, is in substance nothing but the succesion of different political élites. Democracy is a political form that conceals both the conflicts of interest between the governing élite and the governed and the fact that these conflicts are always undemocratically resolved in favor of the former. To the extent that these élites make history, their outstanding leaders are heroes or event-making figures even in a democracy.

The whole force of this argument rests upon a failure

[1] I have previously expounded and criticized the doctrines of this school from a somewhat different point of view in my *Reason, Social Myths and Democracy*, pp. 119 *ff.*, New York, 1940.

to understand the nature of ideals, including political ideals. In addition, the critique overlooks the fact that the problems of political power are always *specific* and that they allow choices between courses of conduct that strengthen or weaken, extend or diminish particular political ideals. Finally, it underestimates the tremendous differences between societies, all of which fall short in varying degrees of the defined ideal of democracy, and the crucial importance of institutions in the never-ending process of realizing ideals.

In virtue of the nature of things and men, no ideal can be perfectly embodied. There is no such thing as absolute health, absolute wisdom, absolute democracy, an absolutely honest man—or an absolutely fat one. Yet when we employ these ideals intelligently we can order a series of flesh and blood men in such a way as to distinguish between them in respect to their being healthier, wiser, or fatter. And so with states. There is no absolutely democratic state, but we can tell when states are more democratic or less democratic. Ideals, in short, are functional. They are principles of organization and reorganization but cannot be identified with any particular organization as it exists at any place and time.

If we define a democratic society as one in which the government rests upon the freely given consent of the governed [1] it is obvious that no society is a perfect democracy, even one in which the members are so few that they can all meet in one place without delegating power to representatives. For we never can be sure that consent

---

[1] For a detailed analysis of this definition, see *ibid.*, p. 285.

is freely given, that is, not in bondage to ignorance, rhetoric, or passion. Further, the division of labor requires that decisions be carried out by individuals and not by the assembly. There can be no guarantee that these decisions as well as the discretionary powers they entail will be carried out in the same spirit as that in which they were authorized.

What follows? That democracy is impossible? No more so than that a man cannot be healthy because he cannot enjoy perfect health. The defects when recognized become problems to be remedied by actions, institutions, checks, and restraints that are themselves informed by the principle or ideal of democracy. The remedies are of course imperfect, fallible, and unguaranteed. But we do not therefore reject them. We continue to improve them—if we are democrats. And we test by the fruits of the process the validity of the unrealizable democratic principle that serves as our functional guide.

Mosca, Pareto, and Michels make much of the fact that when power is delegated in a democracy and when political organizations arise, as they must in a society sufficiently complex, the decisions of the government may reflect the interests of the governors more than the interests of the governed. This is indisputably true.

What follows? Not that democracy is impossible but that it is difficult. It is more difficult under certain social and historical conditions than under others. But as long as we hold to democratic principles, again the remedies consist in thinking up of specific mechanisms, devices, and checks which (1) increase the *participation* of the governed in the processes of government, (2) decrease the *concentrations* of powers—educational, religious, economic, political—in the hands of the governors, and (3) provide for the renewal or withdrawal of the mandates of power by the governed. Again, the remedies may be defective. But if we believe that those whose interests are affected by the policies of government should have a voice in determining those polices, either directly, or indirectly by controlling the makers of policy, the *direction* which the never-ending task of democratizing the social process must take is clear. Whether it does take that direction depends greatly upon us.

That there will always be a governing élite to administer government is true. There will also always be a medical élite to minister to our health. The governing élite will always have more power for good or evil than the medical élite. But it need not be more permanent or even as permanent as the medical élite. So long as the governing élite operates within a framework of a democracy, we have a choice between élites. Where élites must contend with out-élites, the victor must pay a price to the governed for victory. How high the price is depends in part at least on how much the governed ask.[1]

The great limitation of the thought of Mosca, Pareto, and Michels is their failure to appreciate the differential

[1] "For the working masses every 'final victory' proclaimed by their victorious leaders, even if it is a real step forward, can be only another starting point in their endless struggle *for more and always more.*" Max Nomad, in his "Masters—Old and New," *The Making of Society,* edited by V. F. Calverton, p. 892.

advantages of the specific institutions available in a democracy that enable us both to select élites and to curb them. They overlook the concrete ways in which the governed through pressure groups, strikes, public debates, committee hearings, radio discussion, letters and telegrams to newspapers and their representatives, petitions, mass meetings, primaries, and elections actually contribute to moulding the basic policies and decisions of the government in a democracy.[1]

The crux of the issue raised by the contention that democracy is impossible because power is exercised by an organized minority may best be met by asking the following questions: Can a democracy get rid of its ruling élite? Can a democracy rid itself of a governing élite more easily or at a lesser cost than a nondemocratic society? There can hardly be any doubt about the answers. The evidence of politics and history shows that democracy can and has rid itself of governing élites, and that it can do so more easily than is generally possible in nondemocratic societies. That in consequence one élite is replaced by another is a feature of the political process in a complex society, not an indictment of democracy or a proof of its impossibility. Sufficient unto the day is the problem thereof!

Behind the facade of logical argument in the writings of Mosca, Pareto, and Michels are two significant assumptions. The first is that human nature has a fixed and

[1] *Cf.* the brief but excellent discussion of Glenn Morrow in *Ethics,* April 1942, pp. 299 *ff.*; also Arthur Bentley's important but neglected study, *The Process of Government,* Chicago, 1908.

unalterable character from which it can be predicted that democracy in action must fail, not in the innocent sense that a perfect democracy cannot be realized, but in the sense that a working democracy *cannot be bettered* from the standpoint of its own ideal. The second assumption is that the amount of freedom and democracy in a society is determined by a *law already known*. Both assumptions are false.

So far as the position of these social philosophers is based upon the constancy of human nature, their entire political wisdom consists in framing a simple alternative to man—rule or be ruled! But one does not have to be a Utopian to maintain that nothing in human nature limits us to this simple alternative. For other alternatives must be taken together with it. Who is to rule? Over what? For how long? Under what conditions and restrictions? Here is the place for intelligence, experiment, critical adaptation, and political discovery.

The amount and quality of freedom and democracy in a society are determined by many things—economic organization, education, tradition, religion, to name only a few. *But they depend just as much upon our willingness to fight for them as upon any other thing.*

Democracy is difficult, and it is made more difficult because many who call themselves democrats are totalitarians in disguise. The moral is not to call off the struggle but to struggle all the more.

XII *Law, Freedom, and Human Action*

THE UNDERSTANDING of history, like other forms of human evaluation, has its fashions. They range all the way from the view that men are creatures of environment and circumstance to the view that everything is possible to them. Neither of these views can be sustained by evidence. In fact, they are usually so formulated that it is hard to know what would constitute evidence for them. Nonetheless, they have important bearings on the way in which specific problems are approached.

The attitude that man's future is already determined, that the shape of things to come is now settled and cannot be escaped, makes for a slighting of the concrete problems of choice that face us at every turn. On the other hand, the attitude that man can storm the heavens at any historic occasion, that all he needs is a good will or a strong one, leads to a disregard of the limiting conditions of intelligent action. Today the first of these general attitudes is very much in evidence among the opinion makers of the western world. The wave of the future is described as a kind of predetermined fatality that not only will transform our economy but will destroy the last refuges of democratic culture.[1] The drift toward totalitarian political controls is accepted or bemoaned as a natural consequence of the development of our economy and as an inescapable consequence of total war. Those who scoffed at economic determinism during the heyday of capitalism are now become converts to its chief dogma, namely, that the character of a given economic system can determine one, and only one, political and cultural pattern. Although they were able to conceive of capitalism in many political variants, socialism to them seems simply to be what Hitler and Stalin have made of it.

Widespread attitudes and beliefs of this kind have their causes in the objective conditions of the times. But we wish to discuss not the causes of these ideas about history but their validity. What assumptions are involved, and are they true?

*   *   *   *

To begin with, let us note that those who believe that the future of human society is determined by laws *already known* set great store on our knowledge of these laws. It makes a difference, they insist, whether we know

[1] "Like a log on the brink of Niagara Falls we are impelled by unforeseen and irresistible socio-cultural currents, helplessly drifting from one crisis and catastrophe to another." Sorokin, *The Crisis of Our Age*, p. 130, New York, 1941. See also *Cultural and Social Dynamics*, vol. 4, p. 768. A similar mystical view of social fatality is presented in the more influential works of Spengler and Toynbee.

them or ignore them. Why? Because the knowledge of these laws gives us power to direct the future. But this admission means that a considerable area of social history, the area affected by man's knowledge or ignorance, is not determined by the original set of laws but by other laws that come into operation as a consequence of what we know, value, and do. As long as we grant, then, that knowledge makes a difference, we cannot really believe that the future is fixed to a degree where there are no alternatives.

What, after all, shall we understand by historical laws whose iron sway is supposed to determine our future? Roughly speaking, a law in history is a determinate relation between classes of events which we discover can be relied on in solving a problem, overcoming an obstacle, or predicting the future. This covers, however, physical and biological laws, too. Distinctive of historical laws is that the classes of events which they relate, designate the behavior patterns of human beings as members of organized social groups. As members of social groups, the behavior of individuals is marked by ideals, habits, traditions, and other ways of acting associated with the anthropological term "culture."

The subject matter, then, of historical laws always involves reference to the associated, interacting behavior of human beings as members of a society or culture. This remains true even when we seek to explain historical activity by reference to conditions and to events that are themselves controlled by physical laws, like the presence or absence of precious metals or oil in the soil, or the occurrence of drought, floods, and earthquakes. These physical conditions and events have great significance in history and social affairs, but not as physical elements. It is only in relation to some activity or interest of men that they assume significance. That is why the presence of coal and iron and oil in America explains nothing about the history and social life of the American Indians, and so much about the history and social life of the American settlers. "Gold in the ground is a cipher for a study of society so long as we are doing nothing and not tending to do anything in connection with it. Gold that does not exist is an important factor when we are in a turmoil of chasing for it."[1]

The subject matter of historical laws, since it concerns the relations of groups of socially organized human beings to each other, involves reference to human behavior that can be often described by psychological laws. But these psychological laws alone can never explain historical or social events. For historical and social events are determined by the way human beings interact with the physical elements of their environment. Before we can have knowledge of history and society we must have some prior knowledge of nature. Before we can say that it was Brutus who slew Caesar, we must understand something about the biology of death and the physics of the instruments of death. The variable historical and social behavior of men, who are subject to the same psychological laws, indicates that the latter cannot explain the former. Such laws are relevant in history only when

[1] Bentley, *op. cit.*, p. 195.

they are taken together with physical and cultural conditions. "Let desires, skills, purposes, beliefs be what they will, what happens is the product of the interracting intervention of physical conditions like soil, sea, mountains, climate, tools, and machines, in all their vast variety, with the human factor." [1]

Having won the right to consider social and historical laws as relatively autonomous, it remains to ask to what extent they are conditions of human action and to what extent they are modifiable by human action. Let us consider a few typical situations. We present them as purely illustrative of the position to be developed.

1. Suppose a political organization has before it a proposal to nominate a man of Catholic or Jewish faith for the office of President of the United States. It is objected that, although there are no constitutional bars to his election, the history of the country reveals a law of American political behavior that "dooms" him to defeat, despite the fact that in every other aspect he is an ideal candidate. This law states that "no Catholic or Jew can be successful in a race for the highest political office in the United States." It is presented as an induction from experience and fortified by social and psychological generalizations about other aspects of the behavior of American citizens, for instance, their religious traditions and social prejudices.

What is the character of such a "law"? Note that it does not rule out the election of a Catholic or Jew as something literally impossible. It asserts not the impos-

---

[1] John Dewey, *Logic: Theory of Inquiry*, p. 492, New York, 1939.

sibility but the unlikelihood of such an election. Second, the law does not assert that every Protestant will vote against the candidate or that every non-Protestant will vote for him, or that any particular person will vote in this way rather than in that. It states that a sufficient number of Protestants will vote against the candidate solely on the grounds of his religious faith to ensure his defeat. Third, it tells us something about patterns of distribution in a series of human choices or decisions. And we know that human choices or decisions are "influenceable" in certain ways, that they may be changed and modified by changing the conditions under which they have developed. Fourth, its validity is restricted to a certain historical domain. It would be false to apply it to the selection of presidents or prime ministers in countries like England, where the majority of the population is also of the Protestant faith.

Here we have a "law" which every realistic practitioner of politics must take into account. Nonetheless it would be foolish for those responsible for the nomination to accept the law as binding, or even as a decisive guide to action in all cases. The candidate may be a national military hero. His nomination may be pressed on the ground of another "law" that the American people are always grateful to successful military heroes and that they show their gratitude by electing them to office. Under the circumstances, we may believe that the second law will be fulfilled rather than the first. Whichever "law" is invoked, if our decision were based on it alone, we would be assuming that the future of the election is determined by fixed patterns of behavior that have operated in the past. We would be assuming that our decision and the actions following from it made no appreciable difference to the outcome, that the future is determined by the past and not by the past together with the intervening present. In the situation considered, of course, the assumptions would be obviously mistaken. The law that "Catholics and Jews cannot be elected to the highest national office" may cease to be true as a result of changes introduced by our efforts to elect one. The more we know about the conditions under which the attitudes of people have been set, the more intelligently we can go about the task of changing them. If it happens that the country is involved in a war for the survival of its democratic faith, we may go to the country with the demand for an expression of its sincerity in respect to its professed principles. We rely on other laws when we do so, but it is *we* who give them an opportunity to come into operation by the changes in the physical, psychological, and social scene produced by our activities.

We might discover, if our efforts are well organized and if our political campaign is tied into a genuine educational crusade for democracy, that the law "no Catholic or Jew can be President of the United States" holds no more than the "law" which previously had been regarded as just as valid, *viz.*, "no President can be elected to more than two terms of office." We have not abolished the law, but as a result of our action in changing the conditions we have rendered it nugatory. The extent to which our intervention in the present will affect the future outcome, when this is projected as a simple induction from the past, is a matter of degree. In some affairs the future may be accurately predicted with little concern over what we can do about it. In other affairs what we do or leave undone may have more determining significance than any other known factor.

2. Consider another rather different situation. Suppose we were trying to foretell who the next Pope of the Catholic Church will be. We would have to take note of at least the following "laws": (a) "No Protestant or Jew could be Pope." (b) "No Catholic woman could be Pope." (c) "Whoever the Pope was, he would be an Italian Cardinal." None of these laws is certain, but the first is more binding on our prediction than the second, the second more than the third. By this we mean that the chances of electing a non-Italian Catholic man as Pope would be much better than the chances of electing a Catholic woman, and as small as the chances of doing the latter, they would be better than the chances of electing a Protestant or Jew. The reasons are obvious. For the first law to be violated or to cease operating would practically require the entire transformation of the nature of the Church organization and the abandonment of basic theological doctrines. This would be tantamount to virtual dissolution of the Church. At the present time this organization is growing in power. The pressures against which it had to contend in the past are diminishing in intensity, while its own influence on public affairs is growing. Further, without hostile pressure or opposition those who control a successful organization that serves their

interests effectively never liquidate it, or even profoundly modify the doctrines that have been useful to it.

The second law is less binding than the first because if it ceased holding it would not require basic organizational changes but primarily changes in theological doctrine. No longer could the doctrine be accepted that women are a negative element to Holy Orders. And theological changes, as church history eloquently shows, are always easier to make than organizational revolutions. But so far as the calculable future goes, both of these laws are binding upon our prediction. It is extremely improbable that anything that could now be done would lead to their abrogation.

The third law, however, has a different status insofar as the possibility of modifying it is concerned. In the past there have been non-Italian Popes. In the last few centuries we know that Popes have been Italian primarily because of the pressure of the Italian hierarchy. It is easy to see the complications that might ensue if an alien, a citizen of a foreign country with personal and social ties abroad, were to occupy the Holy See and exercise the very real power that a Pope can employ in the internal affairs of Italy. Nonetheless, if Catholic sentiment were organized against existing Italian Fascism, and if the defeat of Italian Fascism were followed by a progressive and democratic regime, the next Pope might well be non-Italian. Out of intelligent self-interest the Catholic hierarchies in countries other than Italy, encouraged by their own governments, might bring influences to bear on the College of Cardinals. Together with the moral pressure of anti-Fascist Italian Catholics on the Italian Cardinals, this might result in the election of a non-Italian Pope. Even if the outcome of activity in this direction were doubtful, the chances of success would not be overwhelmingly unfavorable.

Our next situation is more complicated.

3. In a world where the engines of human destruction are becoming more and more deadly, the problem of preventing war must be met before modern civilization goes down into shambles. Few people profess to enjoy war, everyone deplores its costs, and although the different sides lose unequally in a war, it is questionable whether any long war is economically profitable to anybody. Why then should not the universal acceptance of an absolute pacifism like Tolstoy's be the solution to the problem? Let us grant that if everyone, or almost everyone, actually adopted the Tolstoyian or Gandhian position, war would be impossible. We shall consider the proposal only from the point of view of its efficacy in bringing about the desired results.

It is logically not inconceivable that enough human beings may be converted to pacifist doctrine to prevent wars in the future. But there are so many "laws" of social behavior that would have to be suspended for the doctrine to spread, that the prospect of its adoption must be dismissed as Utopian. Some men will risk their lives because of the intrinsic nobility of an ideal or the truth of a doctrine. But the vast majority of individuals, past and present, have fought for ideals in order to further interests of a more concrete kind, like security, a longer

life, or a materially better one. It is not absolutely ex-
cluded that in time the vast majority of men might be
won to the position of Tolstoy that to be holy is better
than to be, and that to forgive one's enemies is better
than to insist on justice from them. But long before
enough have been converted, the situation will enable
some unpacific men to further their existing interests by
profiting from the nonresisting behavior of those who
practice absolute pacifism. The latter will not fight for
their own lives and possessions or for the lives and possessions of friends, children, and countrymen. In that
case, others, perhaps from countries and regions in which
the ideals of pacifism are held in scorn, will discover that
it is truly to their interest to be aggressively militant and
to cut down and enslave the pacifists. The pacifist argument that it pays everyone not to have wars runs up
against the fact that it would pay some people, in a
world where others were pacifist, to make war on the
pacifists. Consequently, *for the pacifist position to be
truly effective the vast majority of mankind would have
to adopt it at once in order to achieve its universal
benefits.* For until it is adopted by everyone, it pays those
who are not pacifists to reject it. The only kind of war
that is always profitable is a war against pacifists.

What is the chance that everyone, or almost everyone,
would adopt the pacifist position at once? So small that
it would be the height of foolishness to rely upon it in
order to prevent war. The more want, the more bore-
dom, the more fear there is in the world, the smaller the
chance. We must therefore declare that, as a practical

means of preventing war, absolute pacifism is bound to fail, barring a miraculous change in the natures of men in present-day society. It is significant that every absolute pacifist, although he hopes that the propagation of his philosophy will prevent war, will never surrender his philosophy even if he is compelled by the evidence to admit that it cannot be successful. In other words, the ground on which he holds it, ultimately, has nothing to do with its instrumental efficacy in preventing war.

Does this mean that we must accept a law to the effect that there will always be wars between nations and classes in world society? Yes, *if* we accept the major institutions, economic, educational, ethnic, political, that have so far existed in history as permanent features of the social scene. No, *if* we believe that we can use our knowledge of other laws of human behavior to modify these institutions, to experiment and devise new ones, and to correct them in the light of their consequences. *The frequency and intensity of wars can be diminished in a world society in which through peaceful social processes men can actually get at a lesser cost the things they believe—often mistakenly—that war can win for them.* It is not a matter of fate that men must war on one another. Nor are men altogether free not to fight when conflicts of basic interests cannot be resolved to their mutual satisfaction through means other than war.

4. The philosophy and practices of modern democracy to a large extent developed with the growth of a capitalist society. As the capitalist economy matured through the phase of industrial capitalism to finance and

monopoly capitalism, a great many of the freedoms associated with the democratic philosophy became progressively restricted. The economic and social restrictions flowed from the consequences of large-scale industrial organization under capitalism. Political restrictions resulted when the state actively intervened in industry, sometimes to co-operate with, and sometimes to curb, monopolistic practices. Equality of opportunity, central to the philosophy and practice of democracy, was much more in evidence in the agrarian economy of Jefferson's day than in the twentieth-century era of gigantic corporations, trusts, cartels, and monopolies.

Many who are loyal to Jefferson's democratic philosophy believe that it is dying in the present-day capitalist world and that it will certainly be dead in the collectivist world of tomorrow. Unable to convince themselves that his philosophy can be modified so as to vivify and redirect the world of modern industrialism, they urge a return to the earlier agrarian economy, to the simpler capitalist ways of yesterday, as the only material basis upon which the democratic philosophy of life can be restored and defended.

The reply to such proposals is that they are economically *impossible*. The economically *impossible* implies a counter concept of economic *necessity*. What do we understand by economic necessity here, and why is the reply to the agrarian democrats a valid one? What we say will apply *a fortiori* to all proposals which suggest, as a program of action, a return to earlier systems of economy, whose ideals and values we would keep as integral elements of our own democratic philosophy.

Why not, then, go back to an earlier economy? After all, an economic system is a set of social relationships that regulate the behavior of men. It is a scheme of human arrangements, not a God-given or nature-given fact, but something that has resulted historically from the activities of men. True. As a logical possibility we can conceive of any economic system prevailing at any time. But precisely because an economic system is both a *human* economy and a *historical* economy, its basic relations cannot be made over at will.

We could not return to an agrarian economy without destroying our large cities, decentralizing mass-production industries, transforming our banking and transportation systems, producing catastrophic unemployment, making huge plants and many skills obsolescent, and depriving the existing farm population of its market—to mention only a few things. Almost every group in the population would have a vested interest immediately imperiled by the change, and with only the promise of an agrarian Utopia to console them. Even if the promise had a hypnotic effect, the disaster attendant upon any effort to carry out such a program would awaken the populace from their trance. It would require the profoundest modification in present human motives, modes of appreciation, standards of living and taste—all once historically acquired but now set and hardened into habit or second nature. All of men's habits can be altered, but not so many of them at the same time. So long as human beings did not lose their memories, it is even doubtful whether the devastation produced by an earthquake or war would incline them to return to the economies of the past. They would begin to rebuild where they had left off because it would be easier and more "natural" for them to do so. They would choose sites which they believed less subject to earthquakes, or they would turn their cities into impregnable bomb shelters.

The compounding of improbabilities is so great in this projected return to an earlier economy that we call it an *economic impossibility*.

But even suppose the economically "impossible" happened. How could this agrarian economy be stabilized? The free market would still exist. Small commercial enterprises would exist. The human inventive spirit would not remain dormant. New needs would spring up as effects of existing manufacture and as causes of expanding manufacture. There would be wage labor. It would be legally free. The demand for it would make itself felt in the offer of more money than could be made on the farm. An expanding market for the products of industry would be set up. An industrial revolution would begin again. The small cities would become large cities. In short, the agrarian economy would be booming on its way toward industrial capitalism once more.

Left to itself, the social relationships between human beings would acquire, if not the same, then a similar character to that they had when the call for a return to the past was sounded. That is an illustration of what is meant by a *historico-economic necessity*.

But the system would not have to be left to itself! Have we not admitted that a historico-economic necessity is not absolute? True, but in that case, all sorts of controls and restrictions on the glorious freedoms of the agrarian economy would have to be enforced. Those who were so fearful of the encroachment of the state on the freedoms of advanced capitalism would have to encroach just as much on the freedom of the agrarian society in order to prevent it from developing in the way it historically did develop. The philosophy and practice of democracy would be sacrificed for a standard of living which would be lower than the existing standards, and far lower than the potential living standard of an industrialized culture that has not yet lost its democracy.

5. We turn now to the present situation in which the problem is to preserve the democratic way of life, as described in the previous chapter, in an industrial economy moving toward collectivism. This illustration is more topical. If the cultural and political horrors of collectivism as practiced in totalitarian countries of the world were the inescapable concomitants of collectivism, even the futile attempt to return to the agrarian past would be preferable. For the end of such an effort would be death, not the degradation of death-in-life.

The important thing is to determine what is meant by collectivism. Collectivism or socialism can be so defined that the presence of a set of totalitarian techniques of cultural and political rule follows logically from the definition. But we don't have to define it that way. The problem becomes the empirical one of whether these totalitarian techniques in fact would be required for the functioning of such a socialist system.

It would be unfair both to the question and the author to attempt to settle this problem in a few pages, but since we are using it as purely illustrative of our views on law, freedom, and human action it is hoped that allowance will be made for the apparent dogmatism of our remarks.

By a collectivist system we mean one in which the basic instruments of production—the great industries, mines, railroads, utilities, etc.—are owned by the community and operated for public use instead of private profit. This involves a form of planned and continuously planning society in order to provide full employment, equal opportunities of education, and a rising standard of living. The fact that the state or community is the employer gives it a great power over the lives of ordinary citizens since it can deny them access to the use of these instruments. But the state is not an abstraction but a group of men—clerks, bureaucrats, politicians, statesmen, philosophers—call them what you will. What is to prevent them from becoming the dictators of the community if all political and economic and educational power is concentrated in their hands? Nothing, *if* such concentration takes place. For any group of men who had such power would, in fact, be dictators, no matter how benevolent they were!

There are those who say that once collectivism in this sense is introduced we have no longer a genuine *if* but a foregone conclusion. To avoid the conclusion, we have to foreswear collectivism. As opposed to this position it seems to us that the collective control of industry is a "foregone" conclusion, that is, "very probable" independent of our efforts to reverse the trend; whereas the *if*—the total monopoly of power in the hands of the economic planners—depends almost completely upon our faith in democracy and willingness to fight and suffer for it, not only in war but in peace.

The trend toward collectivism in the capitalist economies of all nations in the world is the result of the ever-renewed quest for profit which is at the basis of these systems. The consequence of the quest for profit is the accumulation of huge masses of capital that increase the productive powers of society. At the same time, because of the gross inequalities of income between the different classes engaged in the process of production, the effective purchasing power of the masses for consumers' goods is reduced. The disproportion becomes progressively acute, resulting on the one hand in the narrowing of the field for profitable investment and in large-scale unemployment. More and more the state steps in as a partner in industry and sometimes as independent producer in an attempt to keep production going, to induce new capital investments, and to relieve the growing burden and political dangers of unemployment. Left to the rationale of its own processes, capitalist economy cannot guarantee profits, generate full employment, and provide a standard of living commensurate with the technological potentialities of modern industry. It periodically convulses itself in crises that can only be partially resolved at ever-growing social costs.

The trend toward collectivism and the intervention of the state into economy are "unavoidable." To hark back to the era of free enterprise is just another futile call, of the same kind but not of the same desperate degree as the call to return to an agrarian economy. We can make the attempt, but the overwhelming probability is that we shall disastrously fail. Where our intelligent choice lies is not in trying to contest what seems an irreversible trend but in determining *who* the state shall be, *how* it shall intervene, and the *extent* to which collectivism in production shall go. Therein lies our freedom. Whether in the collectivist economy there will exist certain sectors of private enterprise will be decided by the state. If those who control the state are not interested in preserving the traditional freedoms of democracy, citizens who work in the free sectors will have no greater safeguard from persecution than those who work in the collectivized sector, just as under a Fascist regime professors in private universities have no more freedom of inquiry than professors in public universities. On the other hand, a democratic collectivist society can evolve adequate safeguards against the economic outlawing of heretics by writing into its Bill of Rights the provisions that every citizen has a vested interest in a job, that trade unions, co-operatives, courts, press, churches, and certain institutions of higher education be organized in permanent independence of the state.[1] But whether what is written into a constitution will be enforced in fact again depends upon us. No safeguard can be automatic. That is why freedom is never safe, and intelligence should never slumber.

*   *   *   *

The illustrations considered indicate how we regard the interplay of law and human freedom in social and historical affairs. At any period there are no realistic alternatives to certain paths of development because of the number and cumulative weight of "the laws" that stand in the way of our striking out in a new direction. We may explore theoretically the ideal alternatives *to* this path and lament that we cannot follow them without risking destruction. But in a world where we choose to continue to live, it is wiser to explore the alternatives *on* this path, since it is before these alternatives that we have not only the power to wish but the power to act. No matter what alternative we take, in time we will come to other alternatives, perhaps less ambitious in scope than those we left behind but not necessarily less poignant or meaningful. History and politics, not to speak of personal life, present a daily confrontation of alternatives in which we forge part of our own destiny and for which we therefore assume some responsibility. Every man knows he will die: yet in how many different ways can a man live!

[1] I have briefly discussed some of the safeguards that might be devised in a democratic socialist society. *Op. cit.*, p. 125 *ff.*

There is no complete catalogue of the mistakes men commit when they make history. But in the light of the past we can list the most common among them. They are the failure to see alternatives when they are present; the limitation of alternatives to an oversimplified either-or where more than two are present; false estimates of their relative likelihoods; and, as a special case of this last, a disregard of the effects of our own activity in striving for one rather than another. What these mistakes amount to is a systematic underestimation of man's power to control his future.

The development of societies as well as of individuals along certain lines is sometimes the result of cosmic or earthly accidents. A drought or a tidal wave may undo the planned labor of generations; madness may cloud over the well-cultivated mind before it can reap its golden harvest. Social control and intelligence can mitigate the effects of such contingencies and prevent many of them, but they cannot be eliminated. For man is limited, and the world he can control is much smaller than the world beyond his control. From this no counsel of resignation follows, precisely because these events are accidents. Wise resignation can be made only before what is certain, and, by definition, these events are not.

All genuine opportunities of choice are specific. Every resolution of a choice involves to some degree a reconstruction of the self, society, and the world. Every intelligent reconstruction is an experiment, guided by laws already known, to achieve mastery over concrete problems. To the extent that we are committed to a democratic philosophy, we cannot entrust the present political and social choices before us to an event-making man, or to an uncontrolled élite. As democrats, whatever planning we do must be planning for a free society in which every citizen can participate in the determination of collective policy. Intelligent policies of planning, directed toward the liberation of diversity of talents, can also safeguard the preservation of areas of personal life in which each personality is free to make his own decisions.

Index

Abraham, 8
Accident, Chap. VIII *passim*
Adams, 34
Aeschylus, 29
Ajax, 91
Alexander, 62, 64, 77
Alexandra Feodorovna, 73, 111
Alternatives in History, 7, 114
Anarchisis Cloots, 164
Anti-Semitism, 72
Antonines, 160
Antony, Marc, 177
Aquinas, 32
Aristides, 62
Aristotle, 32, 152
Arnold, Benedict, 132
Assumptions, of determinism, 65 ff.
Ataturk, 51
Augustine, 48, 80, 142
Aurelius, Marcus, 160

Babbitt, Irving, 196
Bach, 30
Bacon, F., 151
Baldwin, S., 4
Balzac, 29
Basle Congress, 18
Bauer, Otto, 227
Beethoven, 30, 35
Belisarius, 164

Belloc, H., 119, 123
Bentley, A., 244
Berkeley, 32
Berkman, Alexander, 226
Berlioz, 30
Bernstein, Martin, 31
Berthier, 98
Bismarck, 131
Blum, Leon, 167
Bolshevik Party, doctrines of, Chap. X *passim*
Booth, 108
Bossuet, 80
Breasted, J., 126
Bruening, 167
Buckle, 61
Buddha, 36
Bukharin, 75
Burckhardt, Jacob, 107
Buturlin, 85, 91

Caesar, 5, 63, 77, 178
Caligula, 162
Calvin, 13, 36
Cantor, 35
Carlyle, 14, 42, 59, 60, 92, 102
Catherine II, 181 ff.
Cattell, J. McKeen, 151
Cezanne, 31
Chamberlain, H. S., 70
Chamberlain, Neville, 171 ff.

Chamberlin, W. H., 213
Chance in History, Chap. VIII
    passim
Charles I, 55, 57, 111
Chernov, 149, 202
Chesterton, G. K., 119
Christ, 36
Christianity, 155 ff.
Churchill, W., 119, 128 ff.
Class Interests and Heroes, 165 ff.
Clemenceau, 133
Cleopatra, 176 ff.
Clerk-Maxwell, 34
Cochrane, C. N., 156
Cohen, M. R., 117, 140
Columbus, 106, 107
Committee of Public Safety, 163
Commodus, 162
Communist International, Chap.
    X *passim*
    purpose, 187
    zig-zag line, 190 ff.
    cooperation with Fascists, 192
Confucius, 36
Constantine, 155 ff.
Contingency, Chap. VIII *passim*
Coolidge, C., 163
Copernicus, 34
Corregio, 31
Correlations between Monarchs
    and Conditions, Chap. III
    passim
Council of Nicea, 165
Cournot, 92, 140
Crébillon, 89
Cromwell, 5, 77, 80, 170
Cunning, of Reason, 61 ff.

Daladier, 171
Dante, 29
Danton, 164
Darwin, 15, 34
David, 31
Debussy, 30
Demetrius, 48

Democracy
    theory of, 230
    heroes in, 232 ff.
    criticism of, 240 ff.
Denikin, 213
Descartes, 32
Determinism, Social, Chap. IV, V
Dewey, John, 104, 238, 250
Dickens, 29
Diderot, 89
Diehl, C., 180
Diocletian, 145
Disraeli, 53
Domitian, 161
Dostoevski, 29
Drouet's cart, 123

Edison, 40
Edward VIII, 11, 105
Einstein, 28, 34
Elizabeth, Empress, 85
Engels, 12, 75, 77, 79 ff.
Ethelbert, 165
Euripides, 29
van Eyck, 31

Faraday, 34
Fascism, 39, 174
February Russian Revolution,
    Chap. X *passim*
Feuerbach, 22
Fisher, H. A. L., 119, 126, Chap.
    VIII *passim*
Ford, 40
Fourier, 34
Frankenstein monster, 69
Frederick II, 67, 73, 85, 92
French Terror, 163
Freud, 93
Fulton, Robert, 124

Galileo, 34
Gametic Interpretation of His-
    tory, Chap. III *passim*
Garner, J. N., 123
George III, 53

Gettysburg, 128
Gibbon, E., 56, 157 ff.
Gibbs, 34
Giotto, 31
Gladstone, 53
Gluck, 30
Goethe, 23, 29
Goldman, Emma, 226
Gould, 9
Greer, D., 163
Guedalia, P., 119
Guizot, 84

Haer, C., 154
Haggin, B. H., 31
Harding, W., 163
Hausset, Madame de, 89
Haydn, 30
Hegel, 32, 49, Chap. IV *passim*, 76, 80, 139
Heroes
  of literature, 29
  of music, 30
  of art, 31
  of philosophy, 32
  of science, 34
  of history, *passim*
  in a democracy, Chap. XI
Hertz, H., 34
Hindemith, 30
Hindenburg, 153, 197
Hitler, 5, 16, 17, 23, 41, 51, 72, 81, 115, 198 ff.
Holmes, O. W., 238
Hoover, H., 4, 123
Hotzsch, O., 183
Hugenberg, A., 197
Hume, 32
Huntington, 93
Huygens, 34

Ideals, regulative, 239
If questions, Chap. VII *passim*
Inevitability, Alleged, 13; Chap. X *passim*
Ingersoll, Robert, 40

James, William, 15, 70, 81
Jefferson, Thomas, 158 ff., 238
Joan of Arc, 91
John, King, 48
Johnson, Andrew, 108
Joseph II, 48
Joyce, 29
Julian, Emperor, 156
July Days in Russia, 206
Justinian, 164 ff., 180

Kamenev, L., 209
Kant, 32
Kautsky, K., 75, 82, 225
Kepler, 34
Kerensky, 149, 202 ff.
Kolchak, 213
Kornilov, 213

Lagrange, 34
Lamprecht, 84
Laplace, 34
Laws in History, Chap. XII *passim*
Leadership, indispensability of, 3
Lee, R. H., 119, 129 ff.
Leibnitz, 32
Lenin, Nicolai, 12, 51, 75, 77, 82, Chap. X *passim*
Leverrier, 34
Liebknecht, Karl, 209
Limitations, of Heroic Action, Chap. VIII *passim*
Lincoln, 108
Liszt, 30
Literacy, as a weapon, 10
Lloyd George, 193
Locke, 32
Louis XIII, 46
Louis XIV, 53
Louis XV, 53, 84, 86, 88
Louis XVI, 53, 94, 111, 112, 124
Louis XVIII, 91, 99
Louisiana Purchase, 159
Long, Huey, 123
Lucretius, 29

Lueger, 72
Lunacharsky, 227
Luther, 13, 36
Luxemburg, Rosa, 209

Magellan, 107
Mani, 36
Marathon, Battle of, 126
 consequences of, 127
Marie Antoinette, 111
Marx, Karl, 12, Chap. V *passim*,
 87, 181
Marxism, Chap. V *passim*
Masaccio, 31
McDougall, 93
Metaxes, 51
Meyer, E., 126
Michels', 240 ff.
Mignet, 84
Miliukov, 202
Milton, 29
Mirabeau, 85
Mohammed, 36
Monarchs, Influence of, Chap. III
Monet, 31
Monod, 84
Montaigne, 6
Montesquieu, 89
Moral responsibility, 148
Morgan, J. P., 9
Morrow, Glenn, 244
Mosca, G., 240 ff.
Moussourgsky, 30
Mozart, 30
Michaelangelo, 31
Munich Pact, 171
Murat, 98
Mussolini, 5, 51

Napoleon, 5, 28, 40, 51, 57, 60, 63,
 67, 73, 77, 82, 85, 98, 103, 124
Necessity in History, Chap. XII
 passim
Nelson, 16
Nero, 162
New Deal, 123

Newton, 34, 104
Nicholas II, 110, 111, 112, 215
Nicholson, H., 119
Nomad, Max, 243

Octavia, 177
Octavian, 177
October Russian Revolution,
 Chap. X *passim*
Ogburn, W. F., 68
Oman, C., 125

Papacy, 253
von Papen, 167
Pareto, V., 240 ff.
Pascal, 176
Paul, 133
Perspective, in History, 137
Peter, the Great, 77
Picasso, 31
Planck, 34
Plato, 24, 32, 152
Plechanov, Chap. V *passim*
Plotinus, 32
Plutarch, 177
Poincaré, Henri, 227
Pompadour, Madame de, 84, 88,
 89, 91, 94, 95, 96
Pompey, 176
Possibility in History, Chap. IX
 passim
Poussin, 31
Proust, 29
Provisional Russian Government,
 Chap. X *passim*

Quesnay, 89

Raphael, 31, 104
Reason in History, 61 ff.
Reichenbach, H., 147
Renouvier, C., 134
Richelieu, 46
Robespierre, 85, 162
Robinson, J. H., 9
Rockefeller, 9

Romulus, 8
Roosevelt, F. D., 118, 123, 147
Rubens, 31

Saint-Beuve, 6, 84
St. Just, 163
Santayana, 21, 133
Schapiro, Meyer, 31
Schleicher, 167
Schoenberg, 30
Shakespeare, 28, 29, 81, 82
Siéyès, Abbé, 86
Slogans, 224
Smith, Alfred, 123
Social Revolutionary Party, 202
Socialism in one country, 188 ff.
Socialist theory, Chap. X *passim*
Socrates, 62
Sophocles, 29
Sorokin, P., 247
Soubise, 84, 86
Soviet-Nazi Pact, 198
Spencer, H., Chap. IV *passim*, 76, 80, 81
Spengler, 61, 139, 247
Spinoza, 32
Squire, J. C., 119
Stalin, J., 5, 23, Chap. X *passim*
    confession of, 204
Stocker, 72
Strauss, 30
Sulla, 145
Suvorov, 85, 91, 92

Taine, 56, 61
Talleyrand, 90
Tarde, 93

Theodora, 178 ff
Thierry, 84
Thyssen, 197
Titian, 31
Tolstoy, 23, 29
Tourtoulon, 117
Toynbee, A., 139, 247
Tree, of History, 134
Trotsky, 51, 75, 77, 110 ff., Chap. X

Uneventful periods, 161

Van Gogh, 31
Van Loon, H., 119
Velasquez, 31
Vespucci, 106, 107
Vico, G., 139
Victoria, Queen, 53
Virgil, 29
Voltaire, 151

Wagner, 30
Wallace, 34
Watteau, 31
Weber, Max, 126
Wells, H. G., 40
Whitman, W., 238
William III, 50
Willkie, W., 118
Wilson, W., 109
Women in history, 175 ff.
Wood, F. A., Chap. III *passim*, 87
World War, 17, 39

Zinoviev, G., 209
Zoroaster, 36